THE GREAT END-TIME DECEPTION

What Every Christian Should Know

EDWARD T. CHAMBERS

Palmetto Publishing Group
Charleston, SC

The Great End-Time Deception
Copyright © 2019 by Edward T. Chambers

Unless otherwise indicated, Bible quotations are taken from the New King James Version of the Bible. Copyright © 1982 by Thomas Nelson, Inc.

First Edition

Printed in the United States

ISBN-13: 978-1-64111-226-0
ISBN-10: 1-64111-226-3

CONTENTS

FIRST THINGS FIRST

Deception in the Church

Now as He sat on the Mount of Olives, the disciples came to Him privately, saying, "Tell us, when will these things be? And what will be the sign of Your coming, and of the end of the age?" And Jesus answered and said to them: "Take heed that no one deceives you. For many will come in My name, saying, 'I am the Christ,' and will deceive many."

—Matthew 24:3–5

When asked about the end times, the first thing Jesus did was warn His closest disciples against deception. Those who are serious about following Jesus should take His warning seriously. In fact, end-time deception is such a problem that Jesus had to tell His closest disciples to be on guard against it. He went on to tell them that many believers would be deceived over this subject. Jesus wasn't just warning us of deception—He was warning us that it will happen! He was telling us that a lot of Christians will get the end times wrong.

Thankfully, our Lord also told us how this deception takes place. He said, "*Many* will come in My name." In other words, it will be popularized by trusted Bible teachers who confess Jesus as their Lord. Our Lord was warning Peter, James, John, and Andrew against being deceived. Like us, they trusted their doctrine from those who believed in Jesus as they did. Peter wouldn't trust the doctrine of a Pharisee, but he might accept a teaching from James or John. That's what makes this deception so dangerous—it comes from trustworthy preachers. Jesus chose to address it first because of the great influence it would have on His followers. I'm convinced it's such an influential deception that I call it the Great End-Time Deception.

How is it possible that so many preachers can be so wrong about the end times? And why will so many in the church simply believe their report? One reason might be the lack of attention given to our Lord's warning. Some are convinced it's a warning for Israel, while many others seem content to believe what is popular. It says a lot when saints are bothered more by their belief being challenged, than they are by their inability to prove what they believe.

Instead of relying upon our own judgment to decide doctrine, we should recognize that God's Word has already decided it. To rely upon our own discernment is prideful. The Scriptures tell us that a haughty or prideful spirit leads to destruction (Prov. 16:18). When Jesus's closest disciples asked Him about the end times, His first response was to warn them of deception. If the first thing they needed was a warning to avoid deception, then it is the first thing we need as well.

Deception: Satan's Greatest Weapon

Now the serpent was more cunning than any other beast of the field which the Lord God had made. And he said to the woman, "Has God indeed said, 'You shall not eat of every tree of the garden'?" And the woman said to the serpent, "We may eat the fruit of the trees of the garden, but of the fruit of the tree which is in the midst of the garden, God has said, 'You shall not eat it, nor shall you touch it lest you die.'" Then the serpent said to the woman, "You will not surely die. For God knows that in the day you eat of it your eyes will be opened, and you will be like God, knowing good and evil."

—Genesis 3:1–5

Deception is the weapon our adversary used to lead us into original sin, and how it happened there in the garden is something we must never forget. It is important to understand that deception occurred after Satan determined that Eve didn't know God's Word. When Eve added "nor shall you touch it" (Gen. 3:3) to God's command to not eat (Gen. 2:17), she added new meaning to what God said. According to her testimony, she could die from touching the fruit, which is something God never said. While her words might seem harmless to some, the reality is that changing God's Word always takes away from its integrity. There is no greater truth than God's Word, so there can be no greater deception than by adding or taking away from it. Eve's addition to God's Word opened the door to that deception.

This tells us that whenever well-meaning preachers add or take away from God's end-time Word, they, too, are opening the door to deception. Our only safeguard is found by staying within the boundaries of God's Word. Staying in the Word also helps us recognize when others are making changes to it. This practice of making changes is so commonplace that it often goes unnoticed. For example, most Christians know Jesus said that He is coming again. But how many have heard a preacher add the two words "for us" to the promise? Those two words change the meaning. Now, instead of Jesus coming, they have Him coming for us. Those two words cause people to think Jesus was talking about *us leaving,* instead of about *Him coming.*

If we are serious about being disciples of Jesus, then we will insist on scriptural verification for everything we believe. Some preachers shrug off Eve adding the phrase "nor touch it" as meaningless and harmless, but that cannot be right, since the Scriptures warn us over and over against adding to the Word (Deut. 4:2; Prov. 30:6; and Rev. 22:18). It's no coincidence that many millennia after the garden, the serpent used the same tactics when questioning Jesus's knowledge of God's Word. While the serpent could deceive Eve, he couldn't deceive Jesus. That's because Eve added to the Word, while Jesus stayed within the Word. This shows us how and when deception occurs, as well as how to avoid it. Adding or taking away from God's Word always opens the door to deception, and the way to avoid it is to stay within the Word.

Religious teachers have a long history of adding to God's Word. Many of them also are unwilling to admit when they are wrong—how else do you explain so many denominations? For some, it is hard to accept that they aren't the experts they make themselves out to be. Religious leaders tried to silence Jesus, but instead of keeping quiet to avoid conflict, He rebuked them! Today's teachers of bad end-time doctrine also need to be spoken up against. The popular end-time doctrine many are preaching is filled with human ideas that change God's Word. And, despite showing just how obvious these changes are, many Christians will continue to believe them over the Word. When Jesus said many deceivers among us will deceive even more of us (Matt. 24:5), He meant it.

I said all that to say that knowing end-time truth isn't for everyone; it's for those seriously committed to following Christ and the Word. It's for those who are committed to growing together as one body in the unity of the faith. Since Jesus said the deception *will* affect many among us, then we have to expect many Christians to be wrong about the end times. Those committed to the truth might even find themselves in the minority.

In chapter 4 of 2 Corinthians, verses 3–4 say that Satan has already blinded the minds of unbelievers, which makes Christians the only ones left for him to deceive. End-time deception is the only church doctrine Jesus warned us about, so end-time doctrine is where we should expect Satan to focus his attack against the church. Those called to fivefold ministry work are instructed to bring the church to the unity of the faith (Eph. 4:13). When such ministers get the coming of Christ right, they make it harder for Satan to scatter the church in our final hour.

Why Deception Is So Dangerous

What makes deception so dangerous is that those infected by it do not know they are infected. That's because deception aggressively promotes itself as the truth. In fact, it must convince people that it is true in order to gain their trust. Once it has convinced a person, it then seeks to turn them into its advocates. These advocates then defend the deception so passionately that they refuse to consider alternative viewpoints. In their mind, they are right, and that is enough for them.

All of us have, at one time or another, convinced ourselves that we were right about something, when we weren't. In fact, we were so convinced that we failed to stop and even consider we might be wrong. Some people (spouse, parent, etc.) probably tried to point out our error, but we wouldn't listen.

Eventually, when the truth got through to us, our eyes were opened, and we recognized we were wrong. That's how deception works. We have all done this, because none of us are immune to it. Deceived people will always resist the thought of being wrong, because deception always convinces people that they are right.

The great end-time deception Jesus warned us about will only happen because a lot of good Christians hold on to their deception as if it were the truth—but being convinced we are right doesn't mean we are. Deception flourishes when we presume to "know" good and evil, as Eve did. Our only safe place is making sure our minds are humble enough to trust what the Word says. If we find ourselves at odds with a scriptural truth, then it will take humility to turn any resistance into compliance. The Scriptures have already decided the truth, and Jesus gave us the Holy Spirit to shine the light on that truth.

The Symptoms

No one knows when they are deceived, but if we pay attention, we might recognize the warning signs. Those signs are: (1) being defensive and over-protective about our doctrine; (2) explaining away Scripture that doesn't agree with us; (3) personal attacks against those who dare to disagree; and (4) using sources outside the Scriptures (such as our favorite preachers, or signs of the times) to justify ourselves. These are all noticeable symptoms that deception is at work.

People deceive themselves all the time. We even grade the various ways it is practiced. We have white lies that many downplay as harmless; we use flattery to lie about liking something that we don't; and we even soften our lies by claiming we just misspoke. While there are many ways humanity practices deception, it all started in the garden, and it is so prevalent that many of its forms have even become acceptable in society.

Deception tries to make us look better than we are, and it offers to protect us. These are the two symptoms to look for when identifying end-time deception: (1) it offers to protect us, and (2) it promises to place us in a better light.

Ask a child how a table lamp got broken, and they might lie to protect themselves from punishment. They would be using deception to protect themselves, and to place themselves in a better light. Adults may embellish talents and experiences to sound more qualified for a job. During a funeral service, people will speak kindly of even the meanest people. During an argument, both husband and wife are convinced the other is more wrong than they, themselves, are. I guarantee you that if both of them focused on their own faults, the argument would cease.

Would it surprise you that there is a popular doctrine that satisfies the two symptoms of deception? It's a doctrine that offers protection (an escape from harmful tribulation) while convincing its believers that they are more spiritual (places them in a better light). I'm talking about the popular rapture teaching.

A lot of Christians have already made up their mind about being raptured, but did you know that there isn't one single Scripture to validate that belief? That's right, not one Scripture, anywhere. Not only that, as with Eve's mistake, I will show that believing in a rapture escape depends upon adding to the Scriptures. God's Word alone is sufficient. His Word should have final authority over our doctrine, and my goal here is to challenge believers to just believe God's Word, and leave off the ideas of man. If you are ready, let's jump in.

CHAPTER 2

OFF WE GO!

The Rapture

*Then we who are alive and remain shall be caught up together with them
in the clouds to meet the Lord in the air.*

—I Thessalonians 4:17

Many believe a time is coming when all believers will vanish from the earth as we are instantly caught up to heaven. This catching away is known as the rapture. It is most common to believe this rapture happens seven years before the Second Coming. It is also the great hope of escape from seven years of great tribulation, the mark of the beast, and the wrath of God. While this belief is definitely more appealing than the prospect of facing great tribulation, the only valid question is whether or not it is scriptural.

I came to Christ in 1983, and can remember well-respected preachers telling us to expect this rapture by 1988. This was based on a Jewish generation being forty years, and 1988 marking the end of the first forty years for the nation of Israel since the time of Jesus. Certain prophecy experts

9

claimed that the Jews reclaiming the land proved they were this generation that Jesus said would not pass away before His words were fulfilled (Matt. 24:34). Those experts were sadly mistaken.

Then, about ten years later, other prophecy preachers began to tie the rapture to the Y2K scare. They warned us that a large number of government and business computers would fail when 1999 ended. They claimed the computers didn't have enough digits in their clocks to recognize the change to a new millennium, and that it would cause worldwide power failures, massive panic, and looting that would give rise to the Antichrist. There was plenty of advertising on Christian radio to buy wood-burning stoves, food in powder form, and sales pitches to convert money into gold for trading purposes. Those Christian prophecy preachers were also sadly mistaken.

Then, about a dozen years after that, end-time excitement was renewed again when another well-respected rapture preacher began suggesting that something significant was going to happen to Israel during the four blood moons of 2014–2015. Israel plays such a vital role during the tribulation for rapture teaching that many of its advocates regard disagreement about Israel as grounds for terminating fellowship. Despite the assertions about the blood moons, this was another false alarm.

What did each of these prophetic mistakes have in common? They were all based on pretribulation teaching. The anticipation stirred up by rapture-believing prophecy experts has so far proven false every time, reminding me of the boy crying wolf when there wasn't one. After thirty-plus years of listening to their predictions, I have never heard even one of them apologize or repent for misleading us. Have you? Revelation 3:19 tells us, "as many as the Lord loves, He rebukes," so why haven't those preachers been rebuked? Why haven't they humbled themselves and apologized?

The subject of the end times has always been a fertile ground for deception, but rapture preachers have taken this deception to new heights. The rapture has so caught the imagination of our generation that fictional movies based on best-selling Christian fictional books are now embraced as biblical. Something is definitely wrong when large numbers of Christians can believe something that strongly without having scriptural proof. Maybe that's why Jesus started His end-time teaching with "Take heed that no one deceives you" (Matt. 24:4).

Most rapture experts tell us this rapture can occur anytime, and without warning, so why are they fascinated by every new warning sign that pops up? The whole idea of their rapture happening unexpectedly means there will not be any warning, so doesn't their fascination with signs suggest they are caught up in *deception*? Serious followers of Jesus will want to steer clear of deception, and the only way to do that is by always verifying what the Word of God really teaches.

A Closer Look!

Look carefully at the following illustration based on 1 Thessalonians 4:16–17, and follow the numbered steps. Does it describe the rapture, or the Second Coming of Christ? This would be easily decided if we were told who changes directions at step 5, but Paul never mentions a change of direction, because he didn't need to. There is no record of Paul previously mentioning a rapture—and the main difference between the rapture and the Second Coming is who changes directions. Those who claim Paul introduced the rapture now have to add a change in direction to the Word of God.

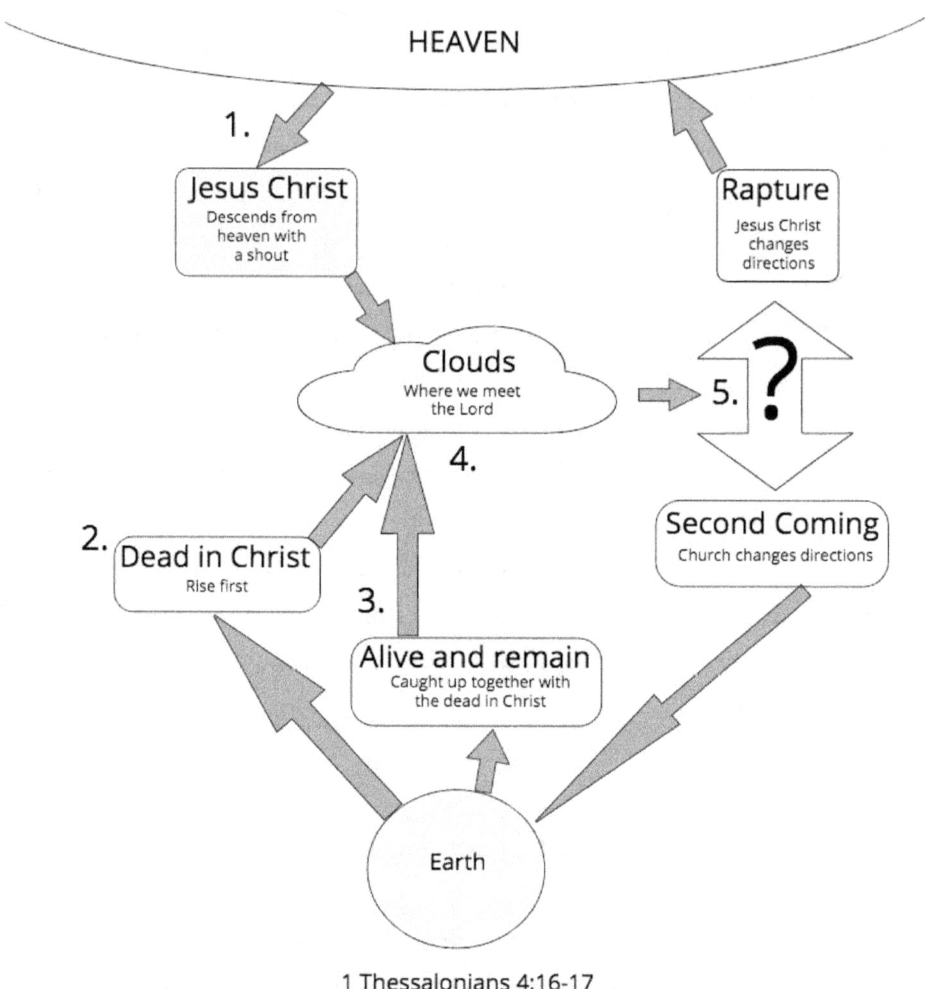

1 Thessalonians 4:16-17
1. For the Lord Himself shall descend from heaven with a shout...
2. And the dead in Christ will rise first.
3. Then we who are alive and remain shall be caught up together with them
4. In the clouds to meet the Lord in the air
5. And thus we shall always be with the Lord. (But where?)

Every serious Bible student believes the church meets the Lord in the air (steps 1 through 4). It's step 5 where the modern church has trouble agreeing. Many believe we are whisked away to heaven in the rapture, without the Scriptures saying that. To conclude that these verses describe a rapture requires us to add new meaning to the text, just as Eve did. We have already seen that the only thing gained by adding to the Scriptures is deception. I would gladly accept the rapture if I could find proof of it in the Scriptures, but I haven't found any, and don't know anyone who has. What is very clear is that Jesus is coming back as He promised.

I used to believe in the rapture many years ago, and tried my best to find it in the Bible. But after meticulously searching and searching, I realized I couldn't find even one verse of Scripture to prove it. This was difficult for me to come to grips with, but I had to because, for me, Scripture alone must decide doctrine. I wanted to believe in the rapture, but I needed biblical proof. I thought there was proof, but tried as I might, I couldn't find it. Don't take my word on this—search the Scriptures for yourself. But as you do, keep in mind that some leading pretribulation teachers even admit there isn't such a verse anywhere in the Bible. In the next chapter, I will quote one of them saying this.

Just because we meet the Lord in the air doesn't mean this isn't the Second Coming. In fact, calling this meeting the rapture is only necessary if it *isn't* the Second Coming. While it cannot be proven that I Thessalonians, chapter 4 describes a rapture, the repeated insistence that it does, seems enough to convince many people that it is.

Different Views

By far, the most popular rapture belief today is the pretribulation view. Going forward, I will refer to it as the "pre-trib" view. This view has become extremely popular in the last hundred years by teaching that the rapture happens before a great tribulation begins. Who among us wouldn't want to skip tribulation? But because of its immense popularity and questionable evidence, it's also the subject of this investigation.

The next largest end-time belief held by Christians is a belief closer to the historic view of the church. This view expects us to endure tribulation right up to the coming of the Lord, and the resurrection of the dead. Pre-trib people like to call this the posttribulation, or "post-trib" view, even though there are some significant differences among Christians in this group.[1] In this group, it isn't necessary to believe in a rapture or a future millennium.

There are other less popular views: the midtribulation view, the pre-wrath view, and the partial-rapture view. The people in these groups believe in a rapture, but they are small in number, and these views don't have enough followers to qualify as "great" end-time deceptions.

What Difference Does It Make?

Some Christians are convinced that it doesn't matter what we believe about the rapture. But would Jesus warn His closest disciples about end-time deception if it wasn't important (Matt. 24:3–5; Mark 13:3–6)? Of course not! Also, because He doesn't want us to be deceived, we should expect to find enough truth in the Word to keep that from happening. Claiming ignorance about this matter is just an excuse to be deceived.

I will show that wrong belief about the rapture can produce believers who, if faced with tribulation, have a higher likelihood of departing from the faith. Furthermore, deception over the end times can lead to other deceptions. Jesus warned that a little leaven from false teachers (Matt. 16:6,

---

1 . For purposes of categorization, I've combined the different beliefs about the millennium—premillennialism, postmillennialism, and amillennialism. All pre-trib believers are also premillennial, so they believe Jesus's Second Coming precedes His literal thousand-year reign. I'm not advocating premillennialism.

11–12; Mark 8:15; Luke 12:1) can result in big changes, so expect error over the end times to pollute our other doctrines.

What If?

By far the most popular end-time view based on TV, radio, and Christian book sales is the pre-trib view. But what if this popular rapture message is completely wrong? The large number of people who believe in it certainly have made it popular enough to qualify for the deception Jesus mentioned. If it was up to us, we would all choose to be raptured, but it isn't up to us— it's up to God. What if instead of being raptured, God's plan was for us to endure tribulation until the Lord returns? I'm not asking you to like it; I'm only asking you what if this is what the Scriptures really teach? If we must endure great tribulation, then what impact would that have on Christians expecting a rapture escape?

If terrorists entered your church and held you at gunpoint, promising to either release you for denying Christ, or kill you for confessing Him, what would you do? What if you had to watch precious loved ones, like your spouse, young children, or grandchildren be killed, or taken into slavery simply because of your faith in Christ? If you expect to be raptured, you might feel confused, and begin to question your faith.

Jesus said that "many" of His followers would grow cold toward Him after facing tough tribulation (Matt. 24:9–12). Those who expect a rapture are more likely to fall away from a tribulation they didn't expect, than people who are expecting one. Rapture believers might get angry with God for allowing such suffering and not rapturing their loved ones. Some of them could become so offended that they would even turn their back on the

Lord. While this kind of persecution seems unlikely to most Americans, it is happening today in other parts of the world.

"But he who endures to the end shall be saved" (Matt. 24:13).

If the pre-trib rapture were true, then it wouldn't matter what we believed about the rapture, because believing in the Lord guarantees that no real believer will be left behind. Scripture tells us "we shall *all* be changed" (I Cor. 15:51), and *all* means *all!* So, if the pre-trib rapture were true, we would all be raptured, and there would be no need to warn us about end-time deception. But He not only warned us; He went on to tell us that we must endure until the end. He never told us we could skip having to endure because of a rapture, and yet that is what many believe will happen. So, we have to choose between believing Jesus, or the preachers telling us we will be raptured. Assuming Jesus is right, those expecting to be raptured will be disappointed, and will be tempted to deny the Lord over their disappointment. Being wrong about a rapture has worse consequences than being wrong about expecting to endure to the end. Those who believe in the rapture had better be able to prove it with the Scriptures, and I don't believe they can!

Proper Attire

Finally, my brethren, be strong in the Lord and in the power of His might. Put on the full armor of God that you may be able to stand against the wiles of the devil.

—Ephesians 6:10–11

If we must endure until the end, those expecting to be raptured will be caught off guard if there is a surprise invasion. Those who believe in a rapture expect to be whisked away to safety to attend the marriage supper of the Lamb before great tribulation breaks out. Most people planning to attend a wedding will dress for the wedding, and not for war. But if the church won't have to endure, then why did Paul tell us to put on the full armor of God (Eph. 6:11)?

Pressing Forward

Jesus Christ is the truth (John 14:6), so if we are committed to following Him, then we will also follow truth wherever it leads us. It's this commitment that keeps us contending for the narrow path, and helps us avoid wandering off into a ditch. Thus, instead of fighting and dividing over concepts like pre-, mid-, or post-, our hunger to know scriptural truth becomes our common ground. The devil knows his time is short. He knows a house divided cannot stand, and he wants to scatter and destroy as many of us as he can. Since day one, he has sought to deceive people regarding the Word of God, so don't let him pull you from your commitment to the truth.

We should always approach the Word of God with humility. We only hurt ourselves by being defensive and resistant to new (to us) light from God's Word. Many in the early church died to make sure the true gospel reached us, so let's at least consider what they believed. They passed along all their important beliefs through their earliest creeds: the Apostles' Creed and the Nicene Creed. Every one of their important doctrines is in those creeds. Both creeds tell us that the Lord will return, and the saints will be resurrected, but both creeds are silent about the rapture—and that silence should speak loudly to us. If the early church believed in a rapture, then we would expect at least some of them to contend for its inclusion in one of the creeds, but they didn't. This means that they never heard of a rapture, or if they did, they didn't take it seriously. Either way, let's see what the evidence of history tells us.

The Arrival of the Rapture Teaching

At the time of this writing, anyone can google "rapture" and read the history of the rapture on Wikipedia.[2] Most unbiased sources agree that we really cannot verify belief in a rapture prior to the sixteenth century. While rapture teachers claim certain statements made by early church leaders show evidence they believed in a rapture, every such argument can be refuted. The popularity of the pre-trib theory has put pressure on rewriting history to include their belief, but their pressure will never overcome the fact that their rapture was excluded from our most important early church creeds. That exclusion is a very good reason for honest truth-seekers to reconsider the alternatives.

The rapture teaching has not just become popular, it's also one of the most aggressively defended doctrines in the church today. Yet there was no such defense of it prior to the sixteenth century. So how did it suddenly become so popular? And why do its advocates fight for it so aggressively? Why do those promoting the rapture teaching refuse to debate it openly in a public forum with those of us who disagree? Why can't the church reach agreement on a common creed? Something supernatural is definitely going on with this rapture, but it isn't scriptural.

---

2 . Wikipedia, s.v. "Rapture," last updated December 30, 2018, 22:39, https://en.wikipedia.org/wiki/Rapture.

CHAPTER 3

WHAT'S NEXT?

Something's Missing!

If you search for a single verse of Scripture which states specifically that the appearing of the Lord Jesus Christ and the catching up of the church is prior to the Tribulation, your search will be in vain. There is no such verse.
—Hilton Sutton, *Rapture: Get Right or Get Left*

I'm not the only one saying there isn't a single Scripture to prove the rapture. The above quote is from Hilton Sutton, a well-respected teacher of the pre-trib rapture. In fairness to him, his argument was meant to suggest that studying the whole Bible was the best way to prove the pre-trib rapture. While he is no longer here to defend himself, other pre-trib experts use a similar argument, claiming the sum of the whole proves their point. Please note that they do this while admitting they don't have a single Scripture to prove what they believe.

But should we believe Bible teachers who claim a doctrine is everywhere in the Bible when they cannot even show it to us in a single verse? Shouldn't their doctrine be decided based on chapter and verse just like every other doctrine? If the decision were up to us, we would choose a rapture escape, but it isn't our choice—it's God's. Our choice is whether we believe Him or not, and the only way to do that is to discover and believe the truth found in His Word. The reason no one has ever found a single Scripture to prove the rapture, and the reason no one ever will, is because there isn't one!

We will not make any real progress until we are willing to admit that there isn't a verse anywhere in any Bible to prove the pre-trib rapture position. In fact, its absence from Scripture should be a loud enough argument against its legitimacy for most people to reject it, but for some reason, it isn't. We know that those hungry for the truth will be able to discover God's truth about the end because Jesus promised that we would, but that means choosing truth, even if it's not popular or comfortable. In other words, we must decide to do God's will above all else: "If anyone wills to do His will, he shall know concerning the doctrine, whether it is from God or whether I speak on My own" (John 7:17).

A while back, I surveyed some pre-trib ministers on Facebook and asked them for their most convincing verse on the pre-trib rapture. These are men of God, whom I respect, and if any of them had proof for the rapture, I would gladly accept it. A few sent me a verse or two commonly used to support rapture teaching, but not one verse proved a rapture. To be fair, I will cover those verses, along with other leading arguments, later on. Most of the pastors agreed with Sutton that they didn't know of such a verse.

While I commend the honesty of the men who knew they couldn't find such a verse, my question is why, then, do they believe in the rapture? How is it that many other Christians also place the same confidence in that doctrine, again without Scripture to prove it? When so many among us place faith in a doctrine without real proof from the Scriptures, something unusual is going on.

What if the reason so many believe in the rapture without proof is that Satan has successfully disguised himself as an angel of light, and is using this doctrine to make his final attack against us more successful? Wouldn't that account for the strong belief without scriptural proof? The Scriptures warn us of a falling away at the end, and what better way to encourage people to lose heart than by giving them a false hope they will never realize? Proverbs 13:12 tells us "hope deferred makes the heart sick," and strong persecution can ruin the faith of those expecting to escape it by a rapture.

Without a single Scripture to stand on, the pre-trib message has grown supernaturally to become the most popular end-time view in the Western church. Many among us haven't considered how or why this happened, and yet we must. Our adversary, the devil, deceives the whole world (Rev. 12:9), and the main thing we should learn from the Garden of Eden is that Satan's deceptive tactics are aimed at changing our perception of the Word of God. When Eve said she would die from touching or eating the forbidden fruit, Satan replied that she wouldn't. So when the Scriptures speak of the last trumpet, it would be Satan-like to suggest it's not the *last* trumpet. When Scripture declares that something happens at the last day, it's Satan-like to say it's not really a day but a much longer period of time. When Scripture calls it the coming of the Lord, it is Satan-like to claim it's really about us leaving.

I will show that pre-trib teaching mimics Satan's behavior by changing "last trumpet," "last day," and "the coming of the Lord" to all mean something different than what is written. Again, something spiritual is definitely going on with this rapture, but it isn't a God thing. Something must fulfill the end-time deception Jesus warned of, and the evidence just keeps mounting against this popular rapture teaching.

Another Jesus

For if he who comes preaches another Jesus whom we have not preached, or if you receive a different spirit which you have not received, or a different gospel which you have not accepted—you may well put up with it!
—2 Corinthians 11:4

In this powerful Scripture, we discover something very disturbing. Here, we learn that the church may be willing to accept another Jesus, a different gospel, and a different spirit. This is alarming and sobering, because instead of rejecting the doctrine of a demon, Paul said the church would yield to a deceptive spirit, and put up with its message. The NLT version says, "You happily put up with whatever anyone tells you." Paul said the church will tolerate teaching from a different spirit—a religious spirit—and we have!

Let me share an experience that was very real and sobering for me.

I believe it was during the spring of 1984, and I had grown frustrated trying to prove the pre-trib view. Tired and weary, I turned on Christian television, looking for encouragement. My ears perked up when the TV preacher shifted his message and began scolding Christians who didn't believe in the rapture. He said those preaching against it were being divisive, and I agreed. He began to plead for unity, and ended his sermon calling on the audience to pray and confess belief in the pre-trib rapture. He said this prayer would remove the confusion and doubt. This couldn't have come at a more vulnerable time for me, and I viewed it as a godsend.

I believed in the rapture, and badly wanted to bring closure to this matter, so I decided I had nothing to lose by repeating the confession after the preacher. It was at that moment when things began to change. As I opened my mouth to begin, I was interrupted by a strong warning from deep within me, warning me there would be no turning back! The experience so moved me that I stopped my confession to ponder its meaning.

It was less than a year before this that God had made Himself more real to me than my own existence, and I knew this was Him speaking to me. As I stood there wondering what it meant, I started to discern a creepy spiritual presence that seemed to be hovering slightly above and in front of me. What I didn't know at that time was that God had opened up the realm of the spirit, and allowed discerning of spirits to operate to help me grasp what was taking place.

Almost immediately, I recognized this presence as the same influence that had been whispering in my ear to believe in the rapture. I also somehow knew that this presence planned to move inside me as I prayed my allegiance to the rapture. Stopping my confession had angered the spirit, and the atmosphere in the room took on an unseen tension that caused the hair on the back of my neck to stand up. Without knowing it, this was a turning point for me. When the presence finally left, I still didn't know what to believe about the rapture, I only knew I had to stay free from that deceptive spirit.

Religious spirits shouldn't scare us, but that doesn't mean we should entertain them. If I had yielded, I might still be blind and in bondage to that spirit, and its doctrinal influence. For me, the blinders would be removed a day or two after this experience, but that might never have happened if the Holy Spirit hadn't graciously warned me that day. Thankfully, I had learned to confess my trust in the Holy Spirit as my guide to the truth, because when I needed Him the most, He showed up and rescued me from my own ignorance. God still sets the captives free, and the anointing still destroys the yoke of bondage (Isa. 10:27). Instead of giving heed to deceptive spirits (1 Tim. 4:1), we should trust God's truth to set us free.

Please notice the contrast between the Jesus of the Bible, and the Jesus of the pre-trib rapture. The Jesus of the Bible promised His disciples tribulation unto death (Matt. 24:9). The Jesus of the Bible told His disciples that salvation included enduring until the end (Matt. 24:13). On the other hand, the pre-trib Jesus plans on rescuing us long before these things happen, and does so without a single Scripture to back him up. While the Jesus of the Bible speaks directly to His own disciples in Matthew, chapter 24, the pre-trib Jesus wants us to believe he is talking to Israel. This pre-trib Jesus is not the Jesus of the Bible; he's another Jesus—and not to be trusted.

Different Gospel

Now about that time Herod the king stretched out his hand to harass some from the church. Then he killed James the brother of John with the sword. And because he saw that it pleased the Jews, he proceeded further to seize Peter also.

—Acts 12:1–3

The true gospel was preached in the midst of great tribulation, and resulted in the deaths of men of God, like Stephen and James. In the very same chapter that Paul warns of a different gospel, he even boasts of his own trials (2 Cor. 11:23–33). On the other hand, the pre-trib gospel boasts of rescuing us before trials get too hard.

Ever since there was a New Testament, the Bible gospel has been preached by those who put their lives on the line. Many have spilled their last drop of blood for Christ as a testimony of what the true gospel looks like. The gospel of the Bible is all about going into all the world, and it has thrived in the midst of great tribulation. The pre-trib gospel can only prosper in countries where there is no serious persecution because it's a different gospel.

Different Spirit

Now the Spirit expressly says that in latter times some will depart from the faith, giving heed to deceiving spirits and doctrines of demons, speaking lies in hypocrisy, having their own conscience seared with a hot iron.

—I Timothy 4:1–2

The pre-trib rapture has a different Jesus than the Bible, and preaches a different gospel than the Bible, because it comes from a different spirit than the Holy Spirit. The Holy Spirit always agrees with the Word, while different spirits always have slightly different points of view. These spirits twist the Word just like the serpent did in the garden. Here is an example exposing such twisting: "Then they will deliver *you* up to tribulation and kill *you*, and *you* will be hated by all nations for My name's sake" (Matt. 24:9).

We know from the context that Jesus delivered this message to His closest disciples, and made it personal for them, using the word "you" three times in the verse. The early disciples were killed for their faith, proving that Jesus spoke the truth. Today, there are parts of the world where His disciples are still killed for their faith, proving that this truth is still relevant. Pre-trib teaching claims these words in Matthew, chapter 24 apply to Israel after the church is raptured, and disregard that Jesus was speaking to His disciples.

Something spiritual is going on, but it isn't scriptural, so it's a different spirit, and probably just like the one I encountered. These different spirits mimic the Holy Spirit while offering alternative meaning to the Scriptures, just like Satan did in the Garden of Eden. A different spirit always makes God's Word mean something *different*, and that's the best way to judge it.

"Beloved, do not believe every spirit, but test the spirits, whether they are of God; because many false prophets have gone out into the world" (I John 4:I).

"My sheep hear My voice, and I know them, and they follow Me" (John I0:27).

We will never discover if there are errors in pre-trib theology if we only listen to pre-trib teaching. Our Lord said we are to hear His voice, and He never said anything about a rapture. Pre-trib scholars admit they don't have a Scripture to prove their rapture, and Jesus never mentioned it, so the logical conclusion is that it isn't the Good Shepherd's voice teaching it. If it isn't the Good Shepherd, then it has to be a different spirit.

The Word of God will never disprove the truth, so if the rapture teaching were true, it would have nothing to fear from the Word. If it were wrong, then it would have everything to fear because the same Word will expose it. We who hear the voice of the Good Shepherd won't reject His Word, so if we find ourselves at odds with Him, then we need to simply change so as to agree with Him. The Holy Spirit never objects to the words of Jesus, and neither will a true disciple. Only a different spirit would tell us Jesus spoke to Israel when the Bible tells us He spoke to His disciples. It's also a different spirit that argues against the ordinary meaning of "last trumpet," "last day," and "coming of the Lord." Different spirits give themselves away by claiming the Word of God is *different* than is plainly written. Testing these spirits is much easier when we genuinely want the truth.

Different Mindset

Many years ago, a youth pastor friend was going through a tough time in his marriage, and confided in me his hope that the rapture would happen soon.

More recently, a Facebook friend facing a struggle wrote that he hoped the rapture would rescue him from his troubles. That they said such things (even jokingly) reveals the escapist mindset held by many expecting to be raptured. We all prefer ease and convenience over pain and suffering, but how much commitment does it take to serve Christ up to a rapture escape? Would such people serve Him if they were told they had to endure tribulation?

"He who endures to the end shall be saved" (Matt. 24:13).

God is full of compassion and mercy, so despite its absence from the Bible, the message "come to Christ, or miss the rapture" does get some people saved. The real Jesus, the one we read of in the Bible, told His closest followers that following Him meant enduring until the end. It takes a stronger commitment to endure persecution and possible death than it does to be raptured. The real voice of the Good Shepherd told His followers they must endure to the end.

Many escapists are so convinced they will be raptured that they cringe at the idea of martyrdom. Would such people have served Christ if they lived during the first three hundred years of the church, when meetings were held in the catacombs to avoid persecution? Tradition tells us that all the original apostles—except for the betrayer Judas, and the beloved John—were martyred for their testimony. Such endurance is still going on today in places far away from the safety of Western civilization.

I'm not advocating we buy tribulation food, get a gun, move to the country, and get off the grid. I am advocating that we show the same courage as the early church, and fight the same good fight of faith. We are the victorious overcoming church of the Lord Jesus Christ, so let's act like it! Our Lord has conquered every enemy, including death itself, so we don't fear what man can do to us. Let's kick the gates of hell down, and rescue as many as we can from Satan's grip!

The Victorious Ones

And they overcame him by the blood of the Lamb and by the word of their testimony, and they did not love their lives to the death.

—Revelation 12:11

Jesus's resurrection demonstrated that He had power over death, and the more we really believe this, the less we will fear it! Most of us in America cannot imagine having to pay with our lives just for preaching the gospel, and yet that was what early believers faced.

Before Jesus ascended to heaven, He told His disciples that their assignment was to be witnesses to Him (Acts 1:8). The Greek word for "witnesses" is also the word for "martyr," and is translated that way in Acts 22:20, when referring to Stephen. This isn't comfortable to talk about, and most of us would prefer not to face martyrdom, but that doesn't change the reality that it has always been a part of real Christianity—even to this day.

The persecution that comes with the true gospel is a big part of why Jesus said we would need the power of the Holy Spirit (Acts 1:8). The power is not just for healing the sick, casting out demons, and raising the dead—it's also for boldly testifying to the world of our victory over death! To hinder the initial spread of Christianity, Satan used the Romans to kill Christians for sport in their coliseums. But instead of deterring the growth of the church, the power of the Holy Spirit through those martyrs led to so many conversions that even the world's mightiest empire had to bow.

In chapter 15 of I Corinthians, verse 19 says, "If in this life only we have hope in Christ, we are of all men the most pitiable". Our lives in this body are temporary, but it's during this time that we choose our eternity. To not choose Christ is just as much an eternal decision as choosing Him. When God raised Jesus from the dead, He provided us with such a great victory that it completely defeated death and the grave. We are not just conquerors, we are more than conquerors! We are such overcomers that even death cannot defeat us. We are the triumphant church, and we have reason to rejoice because we're on the winning side.

Satan wants to deceive the sheep, and turn us into a house divided. Peter, James, Paul, and others, sacrificed their own lives because they shared the real Christ. They testified to the power of the resurrection with their lives. The apostle John so believed that greater is He who is in us, than he that is in the world, that being boiled in oil couldn't quench his faith. These pioneers believed we overcame by the blood of the Lamb, the word of our testimony, and by not loving our lives, even to the death! They didn't fear tribulation, and neither should we. Instead of fearing tribulation, let's understand it better.

CHAPTER 4

UNDERSTANDING TRIBULATION

Tribulation Pursues the Word

The Bible mentions the tribulation from the pressures of life that we all experience. It also tells us that there is a tribulation and anguish that come on every soul that does evil (Rom. 2:9). There is even a verse that says God will repay tribulation on those who cause it upon us (2 Thess. 1:6). But by far, the majority of tribulation Scriptures in the New Testament are directed toward people because of their faith. In fact, more than 70 percent of tribulation Scriptures apply to believers.[3]

Despite the fact that biblical tribulation is usually toward Christians, the allure of the rapture is its promises to escape it before it becomes "great." None of us wants to go through tribulation if we don't have to, but that doesn't mean we get to explain it away. The church fathers endured tribulation unto death without mention of a rapture escape.

---

3 . The Greek word thlipsis is used forty-nine times in the New Testament, with thirty-six applications to the believer, nine to the situation, and four to the sinner.

The apostle Paul, whose writings pre-trib teachers rely heavily upon, also said he was willing to die for Christ (Acts 21:13). While pre-trib teachers confess to being more than conquerors, they are indifferent to confessing such willingness to die for the gospel. Why the inconsistency? Because rapture teaching creates different expectations than the true gospel. The apostle Paul was more than a conqueror, and died in faith to prove it. If pre-trib believers were faced with similar persecution, would they keep preaching the gospel, or would they pray quietly, hoping to escape it?

Pre-trib teachers talk as if being raptured is our goal, but that was not the case for their champion, the apostle Paul. During his fateful trip to Jerusalem, the Scriptures tell us the Holy Spirit testified of chains and tribulations awaiting him in every city along the way. If Paul were making such a journey today, pre-trib believers would certainly remind him of the rapture as a way to escape. But back then, no one did, because the church didn't know about a rapture until much later in history.[4] Instead of looking for a way out of tribulation, Paul tells us very plainly that it was his appointed destiny: "No one should be shaken by these afflictions; for you yourselves know that we are appointed to this. For, in fact, we told you before when we were with you that we would suffer tribulation, just as it happened, and you know" (I Thess. 3:3–4).

What's ironic is that Paul writes of this appointed destiny with tribulation in the same letter in which pre-trib teachers claim he introduces their rapture. Was Paul confused? Did he forget? Maybe he didn't know anything about a rapture escape?

About six years after writing I Thessalonians, we read in Acts 20:22–23 Paul saying, "Now I go bound in the spirit to Jerusalem, not knowing the things that will happen to me there, except that the Holy Spirit testifies

---

4 . Wikipedia, s.v. "Rapture," December 30, 2018.

in every city, saying that chains and tribulation await me." Since this is about six years after writing I Thessalonians, why didn't Paul bring up the rapture here? Despite much time to reconsider this, he still didn't bring it up, because he really didn't know anything about it.

When the prophet Agabus took Paul's belt and bound his own hands to signify what the Holy Spirit said of Paul being bound, the church tried to talk him out of going. Paul's response was not, "I might get raptured." His response was, "I am ready not only to be bound, but also to die at Jerusalem for the name of the Lord" (Acts 21:13). Although Paul welcomed the Holy Spirit's witness of tribulation, I wonder how many Christians today would rebuke such a witness with "God has not appointed me to wrath!"

"And when they had preached the gospel to that city and made many disciples, they returned to Lystra, Iconium, and Antioch, strengthening the souls of the disciples, exhorting them to continue in the faith, and saying, 'We must through many tribulations enter the kingdom of God'" (Acts 14:21–22).

While Paul taught that we must go through many tribulations, rapture preachers tell us we are destined to avoid it. Thus, rapture teaching actually leads people to think in opposition to what the Bible says. Paul also never told Timothy that he might get raptured, instead he told him to endure hardness as a good soldier of Jesus Christ (2 Tim. 2:3). The Word of God is supposed to convict sinners and cause persecution. Jesus said people would either persecute us, or keep His Word. In the book of Revelation, Jesus said lukewarm followers make Him vomit (Rev. 3:15–16). The real Jesus stirred up so much hatred that the crowd voted to have Him killed!

Victory everywhere else means the defeat of our enemy, but victory through the rapture equates to us fleeing from our enemy before he goes on a rampage. While Paul claimed to be more than a conqueror, the rapture teaching justifies cowardly saints. Retreating on a battlefield is considered cowardly, and usually a sign of imminent defeat. There is no greater tribulation than to endure persecution to the point of death, and church history is filled with this greatest of tribulations.

The Why and Who at the End

To learn more about biblical tribulation, let's look at three things Jesus said about it in Mark 4:16–17; John 16:33; and Matthew 24:9, 13.

Let's begin in Mark: "These likewise are the ones sown on stony ground who, when they hear the Word, immediately receive it with gladness; and they have no root in themselves, and so endure only for a time. Afterward, when tribulation or persecution arises for the Word's sake, immediately they stumble" (Mark 4:16–17).

Here, we learn "why" biblical tribulation happens. Jesus said it arises because of the Word. Tribulation in the general sense can affect anyone, but scriptural tribulation is a spiritual attack designed to stop God's Word from working. Nothing is more powerful than the Word of God, and nothing else causes faith to rise or leads to the new birth. There is nothing more devastating to Satan than the Word of God. He knows if he can take the Word from us, he can render us powerless and ineffective. Bible tribulation is like a heat-seeking missile aimed directly at the Word of God.

Next, let's read the account in John: "In the world you will have tribulation; but be of good cheer, I have overcome the world" (John 16:33).

In this second Scripture, Jesus told us that His disciples are the "who" targeted by tribulation. Jesus didn't tell us to be of good cheer because He will rapture us—He told us to expect tribulation. Those who share the Word of God are the targets of tribulation. The Scriptures contain nine times more tribulation references directed toward the believer as toward the unbeliever. Jesus even told us to expect tribulation, so when preachers tell us we get to escape from it, they are contradicting our Lord.

Finally, let's read the verses in Matthew: "Then they will deliver you up to tribulation and kill you, and you will be hated by all nations for My name's sake. . . But he who endures to the end shall be saved" (Matt. 24:9, 13).

In this third account, Jesus brings the "why" and the "who" together during the time of the end. He tells us that His disciples who endure tribulation "until" the end shall be saved. He doesn't say that he who endures until he is rescued shall be saved. According to the Jesus of the Bible, tribulation comes against the Word; we are to expect it in this world; and disciples who endure it until the end will be saved. The things Jesus said about tribulation are completely opposite to the teaching of a great escape. Jesus said His sheep know His voice, and the simplest way to do that is to begin to trust what He said.

We all make mistakes, so if you think I've taken these verses out of context, then please go ahead and try to disprove what I've written. Prove that tribulation doesn't come against the Word; prove that it doesn't come upon disciples while they are in the world; and prove that disciples who endure until the end won't be saved. Go ahead and try, but these are the words of Jesus. Those who believe Jesus Christ has come in the flesh, welcome His words, but those who don't, must reject these words, or misapply them to another people group.

Jesus said that tribulation arises for the Word's sake. That means the tribulation He spoke of has a mission, and that mission is to stop people from sharing God's Word. Biblical tribulation would have no one to attack if we all vanished in the rapture. It has no reason to attack the worldly or the lukewarm because the Word isn't working in their lives. Tribulation attacks God's people, and does so even during the great tribulation: "After these things I looked, and behold, a great multitude which no one could number, of all nations, tribes, peoples, and tongues, standing before the throne and before the Lamb, clothed with white robes, with palm branches in their hands, and crying out with a loud voice, saying, 'Salvation belongs to our God who sits on the throne, and to the Lamb!' Then one of the elders answered, saying to me, 'Who are these arrayed in white robes, and where did they come from?' And I said to him, 'Sir, you know.' So he said to me, 'These are the ones who come out of the great tribulation, and washed their robes and made them white in the blood of the Lamb.'" (Rev. 7:9–10, 13–14).

The people going through this great tribulation have been washed in the blood of the Lamb, and they clearly look like the blood-bought church. But because this is set in the great tribulation, pre-trib teachers will never agree with this. Instead, they have Israel convert to Christ to replace the church during the tribulation. But this can't be true, because Ephesians 1:22–23 tells us that the church is the fullness of Christ. If Christ is made full or complete by the church, then every saved person must be part of that church.

Failure to understand this dynamic relationship that tribulation has with the Word of God is probably the biggest reason people confuse great tribulation with the wrath of God. This confusion has created a big misunderstanding, so let's clear that up.

Tribulation or Wrath

For God did not appoint us to wrath, but to obtain salvation through our
Lord Jesus Christ.

—1 Thessalonians 5:9

Let's assume pre-trib teaching is right, and further assume the church has already been raptured. Then let's assume that you and I were unfortunate enough to be left behind. Could we still get saved during this tribulation period? Of course! Pre-trib teachers even preach this,[5] so there shouldn't be any disagreement on this. Salvation would still have to come through our Lord Jesus Christ. So, if we were saved after being left behind, then according to I Thessalonians 5:9, our salvation should still keep us from the wrath; we either get wrath or salvation—but not both. If someone trusted Christ during the great tribulation, they would still obtain salvation, and still not be appointed to wrath. Some people mistakenly think I Thessalonians 5:9 is contrasting the rapture with tribulation, when it's really contrasting salvation with wrath, and has nothing to do with a rapture.

Instead of changing the meaning of Scripture to agree with our beliefs, we should change our beliefs to agree with the Scriptures. Verse 9 in I Thessalonians, chapter 5 has nothing to do with a rapture. The verse right before it (verse 8) even instructs us to put on the armor of God because we are not appointed to wrath. Soldiers put on armor before facing a battle, not before leaving the battlefield.

Jesus said tribulation comes against those with the Word, and Paul taught that wrath comes against those who refuse the Word. Tribulation and wrath have two very different targets: tribulation is for the saints, while wrath is for the unbeliever.

---

5 . Charles Capps, *End-Time Events: Journey to the End of the Age* (Tulsa, OK: Harrison House Publishers, 2000), 87.

Tribulation and the Falling Away

Jesus also told us that some who receive the Word will only endure until tribulation comes because then they will stumble (Mark 4:16–17). Christians not expecting to endure tribulation will stumble more easily from it than those expecting it, and those planning on being raptured are definitely not expecting tribulation. As this age comes to a close, we should expect Satan to work even harder to cause us to stumble, and deceiving us about tribulation would be a good way to do it.

Jesus told us in Matthew 24:13 that those who endure tribulation until the end shall be saved. It's by holding fast to the Word of God right up to the end that we're able to prove our commitment to Christ. Like those who gave their lives before us, let's not let tribulation keep us from the victory God has provided.

"And they overcame him by the blood of the Lamb and by the word of their testimony, and they did not love their lives to the death" (Rev. 12:11).

Tribulation seeks out the Word to attack it, thus those that want to escape it can do so by keeping quiet about Jesus or by renouncing their faith. In fact, so many will fall away during the last days that the Scriptures warn us often of this (Matt. 24:12; 2 Thess. 2:3; 1 Tim. 4:1; 2 Tim. 4:3-4).

If a rapture were to happen, then God would have to start all over again from scratch. Romans 10:17 tells us that faith comes by hearing, and hearing by the Word, so with the carriers of the Word gone, who would God use? He would have to raise up new preachers and supernaturally train them. They would also have to be so successful and full of the Word as to attract more persecution and tribulation from the Beast of Revelation than the departed church ever attracted from the world.

"Take heed that no one deceives you" (Matt. 24:4).

Perhaps another reason American Christians readily accept a rapture escape is because it fits in with our long history of living free from persecution. While many Christians have suffered persecution, perhaps our lack of it in America has made us oblivious to it. The world hated Jesus, and He said the world will hate those who carry His Word. Just because we've enjoyed great freedom of religion in America doesn't mean we can ignore the truth about persecution in the Scriptures. Instead of promising us a great escape, look at what the real Jesus prayed for us: "I do not pray that You should take them out of the world, but that You should keep them from the evil one" (John 17:15); and "I do not pray for these alone, but also for those who will believe in Me through their word" (John 17:20).

Although being raptured may be the hope of many Christians, the real Jesus specifically prayed against His followers being taken out of the world. Woe to those who prefer the teachings of men over the Word of God! Jesus prayed in agreement with the will of God, and He prayed against a rapture escape. Rather than heeding the teaching of men, let's side with the real Jesus of the Bible and continue to discover what He wanted us to know about the end times.

CHAPTER 5

WHAT JESUS SAID FIRST ABOUT THE END TIMES

To Heed, or Not to Heed

Now as He sat on the Mount of Olives, the disciples came to Him privately, saying, "Tell us, when will these things be? And what will be the sign of Your coming, and of the end of the age?" And Jesus answered and said to them: "Take heed that no one deceives you. For many will come in My name, saying, 'I am the Christ,' and will deceive many."

—Matthew 24:3-5

When Jesus said "take heed," He was telling His disciples to be careful when it came to what they believed about the end times. He warned that we cannot just assume a teacher is right, simply because he teaches in the name of Jesus. If Jesus Christ is Lord, and we wish to avoid deception, then we need to heed His warning. False teachers claim Jesus was speaking to Israel, but they are wrong. Matthew 24:3 tells us plainly that it was His *disciples* who came to Him privately, and it was His disciples who said, "Tell us." Jesus was speaking to disciples, not to Israel.

Imagine someone asks you a question that has no relevance to them. Obviously, the answer applies to someone else, so what would you do? Personally, I would inform them that the answer didn't apply to them, because to not do so would be misleading. Yet pre-trib teachers expect us to believe that Jesus intended His answer to apply to Israel without ever telling His disciples this: "Consistency of interpretation would seem to eliminate any application of this portion of Scripture to the church or the church age, inasmuch as the Lord is dealing with the prophetic program for Israel."[6]

A better guideline for biblical interpretation is to start with "who is being spoken to" and apply it accordingly. We know Jesus was instructing His disciples, so why would pre-trib teachers suggest He wasn't? There is only one answer: deception. When it comes to the end times, Jesus said take heed that no one deceives you, and we need to heed Him on this. Jesus had plenty to say about God's plan for Israel earlier that day in the temple, and what He said there was so important, we will cover it in more detail later. But here, outside the temple, He was privately answering a question asked by a few of His disciples.

By cross-checking Mark's account of this conversation in Matthew, chapter 24, we know Jesus was answering Peter, James, John, and Andrew.[7] In plain English, this means He said to Peter, "Take heed that no one deceives you." He said to James and John, "Take heed that no one deceives you." And He said to Andrew, "Take heed that no one deceives you." He wasn't giving them a prophetic program of Israel; He was warning His closest disciples to be careful about end-time deception.

---

6 . J. Dwight Pentecost, *Things to Come: A Study in Biblical Eschatology* (Grand Rapids, MI: Zondervan, 1965), 278.

7 . Compare Mark 13:3–4 with Matthew 24:3.

By my count, in Matthew, chapter 24, Jesus uses the personal pronoun "you" at least nineteen times, and "your" two times as well.[8] He was speaking to the men He would entrust to pioneer His church. Jesus said His sheep know His voice and follow Him, and He also said we should be careful not to be deceived. There is no evidence that Jesus was warning Israel.

Jesus had already warned His disciples to beware of the leaven (doctrine) of the Pharisees and the Sadducees (Matt. 16:6–12). The Pharisees and Sadducees were the two main sects of the Jewish religion, so any religious instruction the disciples had received likely came from one of these two denominations. The Sadducees were the wealthy sect, and ran the temple, performing its rituals. They ceased to exist after the temple was destroyed in 70 AD. The Pharisees were more popular among the people, and evolved into modern-day Judaism. Both religious groups hated Jesus so much, they conspired to have Him killed.

Jesus never said anything positive about either sect of the Jewish religion, and yet pre-trib theology endorses those practicing the modern-day version. Even though Jesus told them that the kingdom of God would be taken from them, pre-trib theology honors them as God's chosen people. Without Christ, they will be cast into the same hell as anyone else, so if anything, we should be trying to pull them from the flames.

"Therefore I say to you, the kingdom of God will be taken from you and given to a nation bearing the fruits of it" (Matt. 21:43).

The warning in Matthew 24:4 wasn't for the people of Israel who hated Jesus, because they were already deceived. When a person is drowning in water, it's not the time for a lecture on staying out of the water—it's time to throw out a lifeline. The warning is for people in the boat, not for those already drowning.

---

8 . By my count in the NKJV.

Jesus ministered in Israel, and plucked His first disciples from there; that is who He was speaking to. Peter was there when Jesus spoke the words in Matthew, chapter 24, and when Peter preached on the day of Pentecost, he said nothing to Israel about end-time deception; he spoke of their need for salvation in Christ (Acts 2:36, 38). John the Baptist told Israel to repent; Jesus Christ told the people of Israel to repent; and then after the resurrection, Peter told Israel to repent. Do you see a pattern here? The people of Israel didn't need an end-time warning, and they didn't need to be relocated to Israel; they needed to repent!

Some pre-trib pastors are so committed to national Israel's resettlement that they support organizations that relocate Jews back to Israel from places like Russia. The existence of the state of Israel is so important to their eschatology that they would rather quietly help relocate Russian Jews to the land of Israel than to boldly tell them about Jesus. They would rather give them warm blankets than a New Testament. Pre-trib eschatology has so blinded such Christians that they will sacrifice the gospel message to help get Jews back into their homeland! While this may not be true for all, I know pre-trib pastors that it is true for, and maybe you know someone like this too.

Everyone at that private meeting with Jesus (Mark 13:3) was later martyred, except for the apostle John, who we are told survived a deep fry in oil before being left for dead on the island of Patmos. The warning "take heed that no one deceives you" was for followers of Jesus who heeded His words—men like Peter, James, John, and Andrew. If they needed this warning, we need it too. We cannot stop the "many" from being deceived, but we can decide to not be one of them. It starts by heeding this command of our Lord.

Many Will Be Deceived

In Matthew, chapter 24, Jesus's end-time answer was more sobering than encouraging. He was calling for a gut-check by those of us committed to following Him. Rather than speaking of a great revival with "many" getting saved in a great end-time harvest, the "many" Jesus mentions are all negative: He spoke of many deceived, many deceivers, many false prophets, and many that fall away from the faith (Matt. 24:5, 10–12). Jesus warns us of great deception, and the pre-trib response is to tell us He was speaking to someone else? Take heed that no man deceives you.

After warning His church pioneers about this great end-time deception, Jesus mentions nothing of a rapture escape but instead tells them they will be hated and killed for His name's sake. Like I said, His answer was more sobering than encouraging. Today's popular pre-tribulation theory promises a convenient escape never offered by the real Jesus. The real Jesus promised hatred and possible death for those who preached the good news, and His words have proven true time and time again.

Because Jesus said the end-time deception will affect many, we should expect it to affect a significant segment of the body of Christ. The deception will even influence leaders similar in church status to Peter, James, and John. The only way this can happen is for a message to become popular and well-received in the church, and the pre-trib rapture has certainly done that in a relatively short period of time.

Falling Away

Then they will deliver you up to tribulation and kill you, and you will be hated by all nations for My name's sake. And then many will be offended,

*will betray one another, and hate one another. Then many false prophets
will rise up and deceive many. And because lawlessness will abound, the
love of many will grow cold. But he who endures to the end shall be saved.*

—Matthew 24:9–13

Maybe the worst thing about this end-time deception is that it appears to
lead right into a falling away from the faith when things get harder. No one
wants to witness something as horrific as watching their children taken
for slaves after their wife has been raped to death and left in the street, but
there are reports of this happening today in the *Voice of the Martyrs*[9] magazine.
Lawlessness like this would challenge anyone's faith, but it would be doubly
hard for someone expecting Jesus to rescue their family. It is during such
hard times that those expecting a rapture might become offended and grow
cold toward God for not rescuing them. Jesus wasn't the only one connect-
ing end-time deception to a falling away from the faith, as Paul saw the
connection as well: "Let no one deceive you by any means; for that Day will
not come unless the falling away comes first." (2 Thess. 2:3).

Forget the trickery of men who seek to deceive by retranslating this
"falling away" as a departure or catching away. The word used here is the
Greek word *apostasia*, from which we get the English word "apostasy." Any
dictionary will verify that it means a desertion from one's religion. It always
means a departure from faith; it never means a departure from the earth.

In many languages, there are words that come from the same root, and
each word has its own specific meaning. For example: "pneumonia" (in-
flammation of the lungs) and "pneumatic" (air-powered, as in a drill) have
the same root *pneuma* (spirit or God), but each word means something other
than the Spirit of God. "Falling away" doesn't mean "catching away," it

---

9 . A free monthly publication that can be ordered from Persecution.com.

means to depart from the faith. The NAS and Weymouth versions translate the word as "apostasy"; the Williams version translates it as "great revolt"; and Moffat translates it as "the Rebellion." The experts have consistently translated the verse to reflect a falling away from the faith, so don't be misled by any preacher saying the word can also mean a rapture.

When it comes to getting our doctrine right, changing what is written in the Scriptures is unacceptable and off limits. Any doctrine that manipulates the Word of God is a deception. In chapter 2 of 2 Thessalonians, verses 1–3 tell us we will not be gathered (raptured) until the falling away happens first. Jesus told us this falling away occurs because "the love of many will grow cold".

The Big Question

When it came to the disciples' question about the end times, it's significant that the first words out of Jesus's mouth were a warning of deception. Jesus had warned them once before about the doctrine of their Jewish leaders (Matt. 16:6, 12), but this warning was much closer to home because it wasn't a deception by those who hated Him, but a deception by those who claimed to love Him. There was also the sobering promise that many among us shall be deceived. He wasn't just warning His closest disciples that they could be deceived, He was telling them that *many* will be!

Sometimes Christians think being born-again and filled with the Spirit gives us some kind of built-in Holy Spirit radar that makes us immune to deception. Jesus did tell us He will send the Holy Spirit to guide us into all truth and show us things to come (John 16:13), but He still warned about end-time deception! Jesus warned His closest disciples, so end-time deception must be taken seriously.

Playing around with prophecy is dangerous. Deceptive spirits have long been associated with forecasting and predicting the future. Whether it's fortune tellers, palm readers, psychics, or other forms of the occult, they all involve a different spirit than the Holy Spirit. When we allow our imagination to speculate on the future, we are opening the door to deceptive religious spirits. "And no wonder! For Satan himself transforms himself into an angel of light" (2 Cor. 11:14).

The study of Bible prophecy is the one subject where so-called experts can claim to see more than the Word declares and get away with it without having to repent. It's the one doctrine where imagination is often more influential than the Scriptures. It's this vivid use of imagination that accounts for the widespread acceptance of the pre-tribulation rapture. End-time prophecy is the area of the most speculation, the most guesswork, and the most error. There are spirits ready to deceive Christians on the end times by turning the Scriptures into a kind of Ouija, and we shouldn't let our imagination open the door for them. Our path to safety is found in heeding the words of Jesus.

Jesus wasn't just warning His disciples about deception in general; His warning was specific to what they asked about. They asked Him about three things: (1) these things—spoken in and about the temple, (2) the sign of His Coming, and (3) the end of the age. Because they combined these three questions into one, I like to call this "the big question" on the end times. Their big question deserves a big answer.

Not only do pre-trib experts assign the text of Matthew, chapter 24 to Israel, some of them have the audacity to switch the audience back and forth between Israel and the church as it suits them.[10] Such switching tells us they

---

10 . Tim LaHaye, *The Popular Handbook on the Rapture: Experts Speak Out on End-Times Prophecy* (Eugene, OR: Harvest House Publishers, 2012), 55. Chart shows verses 42–44 applying to the rapture, and 29–36 applying to the Second Coming.

are more committed to their doctrine than to the truth. Jesus said the way to know truth is to want it bad enough to "will" it upon ourselves!

"If anyone wills to do His will, he shall know concerning the doctrine, whether it is from God or whether I speak on My own authority" (John 7:17).

We will always quench the Holy Spirit (1 Thess. 5:19) when we rely on human nature to decide doctrine. Although it's natural for us to turn to our own way, the Scriptures tell us that doing so is what leads us astray. What we need to do is transfer that dependence from our own understanding to complete trust in God and His Word.

"All we like sheep have gone astray; we have turned, every one, to his own way" (Isa. 53:6).

"Trust in the Lord with all your heart, and lean not on your own understanding" (Prov. 3:5).

When Jesus said, "Come and follow Me," that is exactly what He meant. This means being fully committed to the fact that God's Word is true, no matter what it teaches us. If we only accept truth that we like, while leaving off what we don't like, we are left with half-truths instead of true doctrine.

Jesus said we would be delivered up to tribulation, with some of us being killed for following Him (Matt. 24:9). This has been happening to His disciples ever since. We don't have to like this truth—we only have to believe it. Jesus knew many would reject what He said about this, and opt for doctrine that is easier on the flesh, but the difference between knowing and not knowing the truth is determined by whose voice we "will" to follow.

Most deceived people are so convinced they are right that they have insulated themselves against recognizing their error. They do not even know they are doing this. Here's how to fix this: Settle it that the Word of God is final authority, and choose to believe it. Begin to replace existing beliefs with the truth of God's Word. Start with acknowledging that Jesus was warning His disciples (Matt. 24:3–4; Mark 13:3–5) and not Israel. Will yourself to do it by faith. In the next chapter, I will help clear this up even further as I point out what Jesus really said to Israel about their future.

CHAPTER 6

THE GREAT END-TIME DECEPTION

The Unholy Trinity

Mark's gospel lets us know that the disciples that met with Jesus in Matthew, chapter 24 were Peter, James, John, and Andrew (Mark 13:3). We know they had questions about three things, and we know what those three things were: (1) the end of the age, (2) the sign of His coming, and (3) "these things." Now we need to consider the context that led to that meeting, because that context determines what they meant by "these things." When we do this, we discover that "these things" were the words Jesus said that day in the temple.

When Jesus answers them, He doesn't specify what part of the question the deception applies to. Thus, it is best to apply it to all three parts. This means we are dealing with a three-pronged deception affecting the end of the age, the sign of His coming, and the things He said that day in the temple. Because there are three potential areas of deception, and because they are connected to one another, I'm calling this three-pronged deception "the great end-time deception."

The disciples' question was so significant that the Lord's answer is now called the Olivet Discourse. It spans some ninety-four verses, starting at Matthew 24:4 and running through to the end of chapter 25. Jesus began His answer with a warning to help us guard ourselves from misunderstanding the rest of His answer.

Of all the church doctrines, this is the only one Jesus issued such a warning about. That tells us that Jesus expected more believers to be caught up by false teaching about the end times than by any other doctrine. And because it is a three-pronged deception, we should expect this deception to influence all three parts of the question, making for an entangled mess.

Here is how that entanglement works: Challenge one of the three areas of deception, and the deceived person can simply dismiss the challenge because they cannot reconcile it with what they believe about one of the other two areas. For example, they can reject a teaching about the coming of the Lord, not because it isn't in the Bible, but because it doesn't fit with what they believe about the end of the age. Likewise, the deceived person can reject what the Bible says happens at the last day, not because it isn't in the Bible, but because it doesn't fit with their belief about the coming of the Lord. Thus, their deception about one part of the question keeps them from discovering the truth about the other parts.

Thankfully, Jesus taught us how to recognize the deception. He first gave us a summary overview that serves as the boundaries for the details that followed. That overview is found in Matthew 24:4–14, and any end-time doctrine that doesn't fit into this summary is wrong and deceptive. Giving the boundaries first helps us keep everything else in proper context.

Now let's take a closer look at each of the three parts of the question, beginning with "these things." Luke 21:7 tells us that it was "these things" that prompted their question.

These Things

Now as He sat on the Mount of Olives, the disciples came to Him privately, saying, "Tell us, when will these things be?"

—Matthew 24:3

What things were they referring to? They were referring to the condemning rebuke He had just given the leaders of the Jewish religion before leaving the temple. He so infuriated those religious leaders that they would have Him killed within forty-eight hours. When He finished rebuking the temple leaders and their religion, His last remark before leaving was to let them know that He was done with them until they recognized Him as Messiah (Matt. 23:37–39).

His disciples must have been in shock. Instead of Messiah taking over Israel, He had just signed His death warrant. As He was leaving the temple, some of the disciples pointed to the beauty of the buildings. Surely Jesus could use some of them for His kingdom. His reply only reinforced what He had just said in the temple: "Do you not see all these things? Assuredly, I say to you, not one stone shall be left here upon another, that shall not be thrown down" (Matt. 24:2).

Jesus made the point that God no longer needed the Jewish religion or their temple. His disciples were hearing something very hard for them to swallow. "These things" troubled them, and would confuse them for many years after this. This is because they thought the kingdom was about

Israel, but it turned out to be about the Christ. Israel wasn't the promised seed of Abraham after all, because that seed was Jesus (Gal. 3:16). He was their promised Messiah and their final Passover sacrifice. He was the reason Israel was chosen by God. He was the Word made flesh. He was what the Scriptures were always about.

The temple had long been the centerpiece of the Jewish religion, and had been undergoing restoration for some forty-six years (John 2:20). Coincidentally, that restoration began under Herod the Great—the same Herod who slaughtered the male babies in Bethlehem while attempting to kill the young Jesus (Matt. 2:16).

Israel's temple was part of their religious identity, so hearing Jesus say that it would be destroyed was confusing and disturbing to them. It was just after saying this that Peter, James, John, and Andrew, came to Jesus privately (Mark 13:3). While we may never know why only four disciples came to Jesus, what we do know is that a better understanding of "these things" helps us understand Jesus's answer. Let's look closer.

A Closer Look

Jesus entered the temple that day, and had just started teaching when the chief priests and elders confronted Him. They didn't just question His authority to teach, they questioned His authority regarding the things He had been doing (Matt. 21:23). It was just the day before when He caused a ruckus at this same temple. He had turned over the tables of the money changers and done nothing to silence the multitudes when they'd cried out to Him as "the Son of David." Coincidentally, this same multitude that acknowledged Him as the Son of David would cry, "Crucify Him!" just two days later.

It was the charge of claiming to be the Christ that got Him condemned (Mark 14:61–64), but don't overlook His charge against them of turning His house of prayer into a den of thieves. The merchants couldn't carry on business in the temple without some kind of financial agreement with the temple authorities, so Jesus was condemning the entire religious system of the Jewish people there at their most sacred place. Condemning their temple by calling it a den of thieves made Him their enemy, and a threat to their religion.

That next day, when the chief priests approached Him, they were upset He had allowed people to acknowledge Him as Messiah, and that He dared to judge their religious practices, so they asked about His authority. Today's version might sound something like, "Just who do you think you are, coming in here acting like this?" So, it was on this next day, inside Herod's temple (the same day He would deliver the Olivet Discourse), that their own Messiah would tell them and us what He really thought of them, and their religion. What He said was such a game changer that only the four closest of Jesus's disciples would dare ask Him about it. Understanding what happened that day gives us the proper perspective for Jesus's answer.

It began with the chief priests trying to get Jesus to incriminate Himself, but they got more than they bargained for. Beginning at their question in Matthew 21:23, all the way through chapters 22 and 23, Jesus gave what reads as a non-stop condemnation. It's no wonder the chief priests made haste to have Him killed shortly afterward. They were the recognized temple authorities, and like many religious leaders, thought more highly of themselves than they ought to have, and believed they had a right to question Jesus's authority. The Lord offered to answer them if they answered one question He had, but their spiritual pride got in the way of their answer, so He told them a few parables instead.

The way Jesus spoke to the religious leaders of Israel would be considered offensive speech today. Instead of offering suggestions for bridging the gap between Judaism and Christianity, He told the temple leaders that "harlots shall enter the kingdom of God before you" (Matt. 21:31). Try to imagine a Catholic priest visiting the Vatican and suggesting to its leadership that local prostitutes had a better chance of getting to heaven than them. Jesus was insulting the high priests in a way that no Jew had ever dared to do, and He was just getting started! He then told them another parable, and you won't believe what He said, unless you read it for yourself: "Therefore I say to you, the kingdom of God will be taken from you and given to a nation bearing the fruits of it" (Matt. 21:43).

Jesus Christ dared to tell these Jewish leaders that the kingdom of God was being taken from them and given to another nation. He didn't say God's kingdom was being given to another Jewish sect, or to another Jewish priesthood—He said it was going to another "nation" altogether. He was telling the same people who had been chosen to bring God's promise to pass that they were no longer needed!

This was a pivotal time in Israel's history. Here was their promised Messiah, standing in their temple, rejecting their religion, and telling them that the kingdom of God was leaving their nation. Here was God's Son, telling them they were being fired! Those who fail to grasp the significance of what happened that day will continue to confuse natural Israel with God's Israel (Rom. 9:6–8).

When prophetic teachers declare that God will resume His dealings with Israel during the tribulation period, they have failed to account for what happened that day in the temple. Jesus's words so angered the religious leaders that they turned on their own Messiah and made Him their once-for-all-time sacrificial lamb without even knowing it. It's no wonder Paul wrote of the foolishness of God being wiser than the wisdom of man (I Cor. I:25)!

Did Jesus lie about the kingdom of God being taken from Israel? Look at Matthew 21:43 and tell me He didn't say that. Did He ever mention restoring the kingdom back to Israel? No, He never did! So, why do pre-trib teachers not see this? Maybe they don't want to see it. At least they can take solace in knowing that the twelve also had trouble understanding the move to this other nation.

In Acts, chapter I, after Jesus was resurrected, the disciples asked Him about restoring the kingdom to Israel. He had just spent forty days talking to them about the kingdom of God (Acts I:3), and here they were, still trying to relate everything to a different kingdom—the kingdom of Israel. Jesus answered by telling them that times and seasons were not for them to know (Acts I:6–7). They were not supposed to try and figure such things out, and yet that's what pre-trib teaching must do to substantiate their claims about a future kingdom of Israel. Jesus said such things weren't for us to know, so either Jesus is right, or pre-trib teaching is right. Jesus never justified an answer about the restoration of Israel, so that should tell us that the subject isn't relevant, and should be left alone. He is the rock of our salvation, and we follow Him. He said the kingdom of God will be taken from Israel, and we should just agree that it has.

In fairness, the words Jesus spoke that day in the temple were tough for His closest followers to swallow. They expected Messiah to come in power and rescue Israel; they didn't expect Him to tear their nation and religion apart. The people of Israel had been told for so long that they were God's chosen people, they probably never realized what God meant by that. What they didn't realize, and remains somewhat of a mystery even to this day, was that God's Israel was different than man's Israel.[11]

In Matthew, chapter 22, on three separate occasions, the Jews send Pharisees, Sadducees, and even a lawyer to try and catch Jesus in a misstatement, but the wisdom of God in Him silenced them all (Matt. 22:46). Then, in chapter 23, Jesus tears into the religious leaders and their followers, using more "woes" than any other chapter in the entire Bible! No wonder the Jewish leaders had Him arrested within forty-eight hours.

The chain of events that day in the temple helps us understand why only a few key disciples came to Him privately with questions about "these things." It was "these things" that were the straw that broke the camel's back and led to His crucifixion. It was "these things" that angered the chief priests and elders enough to persuade the multitude to ask for the release of Barabbas (Matt. 27:20), and it was "these things" that sparked the big question asked by the disciples.

His words that day in the temple were His last words to the nation of Israel. He went after the lost sheep of Israel, giving as many as possible a chance to get onboard with God's plan, but just like most people today, the majority wanted God on their terms rather than His. God had sent them prophet after prophet that they killed, and now He had sent them His Son. But rather than accepting God's Son, they would kill Him. Jesus knew all this as He spoke the final words of His final message to them: "O Jerusalem, Jerusalem, the one who kills the prophets and stones those who are sent to her! How often I wanted to gather your children together,

---

11 . Romans 9:6 tells us there are two different Israels. To help us better understand this, in Romans 9:7–8, Paul explains the real meaning of the seed of Abraham before contrasting the two Israels as: (1) the children of the flesh, and (2) the children of the promise. He writes that only children of the promise are the children of God. Paul tells us who these children of promise are in Galatians 4:28, where we discover that Christians, regardless of whether Gentile or Jew, are these children. Although it's a mystery (Eph. 3:3–11), Paul taught us God's Israel became the church (Eph. 2:11–16; Gal. 6:15–16).

as a hen gathers her chicks under her wings, but you were not willing! See! Your house is left to you desolate; for I say to you, you shall see Me no more till you say, 'Blessed is He who comes in the name of the Lord!'" (Matt. 23:37–39).

After these sobering words, He walked out of the temple knowing the next time they saw Him they would arrest Him so they could kill Him. It was "these things" He said that day in the temple that led to the private meeting with Peter, James, John, and Andrew. It was "these things" they wanted to know about, and it was "these things" that caused them to ask about the sign of His coming and the end of the age. Misunderstanding "these things" is the foundation for the great end-time deception.

CHAPTER 7

THE SIGN OF HIS COMING

His disciples were expecting Jesus to claim His throne as Messiah, so when He announced the kingdom of God was leaving Israel for another nation, they needed time to process what He meant by that. What Jesus said made them uncertain about what to look for regarding His coming, so they asked Him about it.

Looking for Signs Everywhere

Now as He sat on the Mount of Olives, the disciples came to Him privately, saying, "Tell us, when will these things be? And what will be the sign of Your coming, and of the end of the age?"

—Matthew 24:3

Signs were a familiar part of their Jewish religion, and considered evidence of God's involvement. The sign of circumcision (Gen. 17:11) was evidence of the Abrahamic covenant. The blood on the doorpost during the first Passover was the sign God would pass over their sins (Exod. 12:13). God even told them about the sign of a virgin bearing a son (Isa. 7:14) some seven hundred years before it happened. Most Jews, even today, fail to recognize that last sign. As Jesus answered His disciples, He warned them of false prophets who would use great signs and wonders to deceive (Matt. 24:11, 24). Let's talk about several such signs.

We have already mentioned how the rebirth of Israel in 1948 was such a prominent sign for pre-trib believers that many of them were convinced they would be raptured before 1988. But did you know that Jews have always wanted to return to their land of promise? They believe a substantial portion of their Jewish law can only be performed in the land of Israel. Their Talmud[12] even promises them that walking in the land of Israel gives them a place in the world to come.[13] Since officially rejecting their Messiah, many have turned their hope to the promised land of Israel, and it's that hope that led to their retaking of it in 1948. It's ironic that they expect God to bless them for possessing the land promised to Abraham, while they continue to reject his Seed (Jesus the Messiah).

Some pre-trib teachers take the return to the land of Israel as the greatest "sign" we are living in the time of the end, some even watch Israel as if it were God's time clock. But Jesus never said to watch Israel, He said the kingdom of God will be taken from them, and their house would be left to them desolate.

Instead of recognizing that the majority of Jewish Israel turned their back on God by rejecting His Son, the pre-trib camp warns that our nation must defend Israel or lose God's blessing. While Israel is an ally we should defend, our blessings are secured in Christ (2 Cor. 1:20). Pre-trib teachers also instruct the church to pray for the peace of Jerusalem as if doing so keeps us in God's favor. There can be no peace for Jerusalem apart from the Prince of Peace, and anyone who says otherwise is deceived.

---

12 The Talmud is the record of rabbinic teachings spanning about six hundred years, from the first century CE. through the sixth and seventh centuries CE. *Talmud* is Hebrew for "study," or "instruction."
13 http://www.jewfaq.org/Israel.htm#Promised

Jesus said false prophets would use false signs to deceive people, and some of those signs could even deceive the elect (Matt. 24:24). Deceptive signs can be a heavenly or earthly phenomenon like the four blood moons, the Y2K scare, or the rebirth of the Jewish nation. Each of these "signs" has already fooled many who claim Christ Jesus as Lord.

While most of us think deception is something that affects someone else, the truth is, none of us are immune to it. The subject of the coming of the Lord is problematic, and a lot of good Christians are being misinformed, just as Jesus said they would be. Many people cling to such signs without letting the Word of God correct them. Perhaps we could help with a wake-up call, so let's investigate something that's become a sort of sacred cow for some of them—the third temple.

The Third Temple

While pre-trib eschatology claims the rapture can happen without warning, they also need an existing temple in Jerusalem for the Antichrist to perform the abomination of desolation (Matt. 24:15-16; Dan. 11:31). Thus, they considered the rebirth of the nation of Israel in 1948 a major sign that we are closer to the end of the age. But how could a sign legitimize an event that they claim happens without a sign? It can't, but it can be used to mislead people.

Let's summarize the pre-trib timeline: First, the church must be raptured, and next, the Antichrist must immediately make a seven-year agreement with Israel. Then Israel must quickly rebuild their temple so the Antichrist can destroy it by the middle of these seven years (Dan. 9:27). Pre-trib teaching calls this seven-year period the great tribulation. Without the people in Israel ready to build a temple, this could never work.

Pre-trib teachers have this story all worked out nicely to fit within their timeline, but it doesn't fit with reality. Solomon's temple took seven years to build (1 Kings 6:38) during a time of great peace, and only after huge resources had been stockpiled by King David. The second temple took forty-six years to rebuild (John 2:20) during less favorable times. The current situation today in Jerusalem is far more complicated than when the second temple was built.

In AD 691, the religion of Islam built the Dome of the Rock on top of the temple mount where the Jewish temple is supposed to be rebuilt. Although it had a brief collapse that was rebuilt, the Dome of the Rock has remained there until this day. Demolishing the Dome to rebuild a Jewish temple would be met with great repercussion by most in the international community. The Antichrist would have to work a miracle to get the Islamic people to agree to both the destruction of their Dome, and to allow a rebuild of the Jewish temple. If we were raptured *today*, does anyone really believe the world is ready for such a rebuild anytime soon? Yet, the third temple can only be rebuilt after an agreement is negotiated with the international Islamic community. Such negotiations with Islam, and the subsequent rebuilding of the temple, would both have to be done in less than three and a half years after we vanish, and that's half the time it took to build Solomon's temple. Factor in the long-standing feud between Islam and the Jews, and it's highly improbable this will ever happen.

"Watch therefore, for you know neither the day nor the hour in which the Son of Man is *coming*" (Matt. 25:13).

There are scriptural problems for a rebuilt temple as well. If the temple must be rebuilt before Jesus returns, we would have no reason to watch for His coming before then. Pre-trib teachers work around this by telling us Jesus was talking about the rapture, and not the Second Coming. They may say this, but in the verse above, Jesus said He was coming.

The rapture involves the church vanishing to heaven, while His coming means He is coming here. Matthew 25:13 says nothing about us leaving, but it does tell us "the Son of Man is coming." To make this verse about us leaving requires twisting the meaning of the Scripture. Using the term "rapture" conjures imaginations of us leaving, and helps take our mind off what Jesus said about "coming." Deception is sneaky!

If pre-trib teaching were to follow through on their interpretation of the abomination of Daniel, then Jesus will come either 1,290 days, or 1,335 days after the destruction of the third temple.[14] Thus, if they were right about the tribulation, then we would also know the day Jesus was returning. They would never admit to knowing that day because that would mean they believe our Lord lied. We all agree that Jesus didn't lie to us, but that also means He didn't lie when He said He was coming.

An Alternative View

The same day Jesus walked out of the temple and prophesied its destruction was the same day He spoke of the abomination of desolation. So why couldn't it be as simple as Jesus telling Peter, James, and John about that existing temple? He was, after all, speaking to them. That temple was destroyed in AD 70, and happened within a generation (Matt. 24:34), just as Jesus prophesied. Most Christian Jews had already fled Jerusalem as Jesus warned them to do (Luke 21:20–24) even before the Jewish Revolt of AD 66, which led to an ongoing war with the Romans.

---

14 . Compare Daniel 9:27 with Daniel 12:11–12.

Eusebius wrote that by the time the revolt began, many of the remaining Christians had already been warned, and fled to Pella.[15] A Roman siege took place, and the war continued on and off for about seven years, until AD 73,[16] which is the length of time pre-trib teachers use for their future great tribulation.

Around the middle of those seven years during AD 70, the remaining Jews of Jerusalem had no recourse but to retreat inside the temple, where they were massacred or taken as slaves. Their temple was destroyed and burned by Roman soldiers a little more than three and a half years after this great tribulation started. Prior to 1948, most Christians considered this desecration of the temple in AD 70 to be the abomination of desolation.

It's also important to point out that Revelation 11:1 calls its temple the "temple of God." Jesus said that no one can come to the Father except through Him (John 14:6), so any temple that doesn't honor Him cannot be God's. The second temple was no longer God's temple when it was destroyed because Jesus rejected it and left it to the Jews desolate (Matt. 23:38). When Jesus walked out, it was no longer God's temple.

"Destroy this temple, and in three days I will raise it up" (John 2:19).

Jesus introduced the revelation that His body would become the new temple. Paul taught us that the church is now the body of Christ (1 Cor. 12:27; Eph. 1:22–23) and the temple of God (1 Cor. 3:16–17; 2 Cor. 6:16). The New Covenant brought in a big change regarding the temple of God, as it is no longer a building made by hand.

In the New Testament, Paul also told us that the man of sin sits as God in the "temple of God" (2 Thess. 2:4). Because this was written before the

---

15 . Wikipedia, s.v. "Flight to Pella," last modified October 24, 2018, 17:19, https://en.wikipedia.org/wiki/Flight_to_Pella.

16 . Wikipedia, s.v. "First Jewish-Roman War," last modified March 6, 2019, 19:38, https://en.wikipedia.org/wiki/First_Jewish-Roman_War.

destruction of the second temple, there is some uncertainty here, but if it's in the future, then it wouldn't qualify as God's temple if it was used for sin sacrifices. The best we could say about such a future temple with animal sacrifices is to call it a Jewish temple, while the worst would be to call it a synagogue of Satan (Rev. 3:9). Pre-trib teaching about a future temple is based on Old Testament understanding, and completely ignores what the New Testament tells us God's temple became.

Pick Your Favorite Color

A case can certainly be made for a future temple. Jesus said He would come on the clouds immediately after the tribulation of those days, and that hasn't happened yet. Those who literalize the destruction of the temple in AD 70 cannot now spiritualize this part of the text. The fact remains that Jesus hasn't returned, and He will! Also, Revelation 11:1–2 speaks of the temple of God, and the time of the Gentiles treading the holy city underfoot for forty-two months; most scholars suggest this was written many years after the second temple had been destroyed.

When it comes to the abomination of desolation, the most honest answer is that both those who believe in a future temple, and those who believe it happened in AD 70, have Scripture to argue their position, and both have Scripture that seems to contradict them. When I step back and observe such arguments, it doesn't seem much different to me than two children arguing over what color is the best color. In other words, it's not worth arguing about.

"This is an evil generation. It seeks a sign" (Luke 11:29).

The only sign Jesus said His generation would receive is the sign of Jonah the prophet, and that's the same sign we have today. Tongues are a sign to the unbeliever (1 Cor. 14:22), but the cross and resurrection are the only signs that can transform a life and turn it into the temple of God. When we believe God raised Jesus from the dead and confess He is Lord, He changes us into new creatures, and instead of chasing signs, we get to demonstrate them (Mark 16:17, 20; Acts 4:30, 5:12, 8:13, 14:3; Rom. 15:19; 2 Cor. 12:12). Although the disciples didn't understand this when they asked about His coming, they eventually learned to stop looking for signs and to focus on preaching the gospel.

After the resurrection but before His ascension, our Lord told us specifically to avoid speculating on signs of the times: "It is not for you to know times or seasons which the Father has put in His own authority" (Acts 1:7). So, while false prophecy teachers point their followers to supposed prophetic clues in the current times and seasons, Jesus said it's wrong to even look for such clues. The main point about trying to understand the abomination is that we should quit trying because it's still not for us to know times or seasons, and there's no sense arguing which color is best.

Observing Versus Speculating

Observing signs is different than speculating about those signs. Observing a sign involves nothing predictive because all we are doing is observing God's Word coming to pass. That is the right way to observe the signs of the times. Speculations, on the other hand, involve man's predictions about those signs. Speculating is guessing how signs will play out or how they will come to pass. Jesus said no one knows the day nor the hour, not even Him, so it is worse than foolish to get caught up in such speculations—it is the playground of deceptive spirits. The best answer when we do not see something clearly in the Scriptures is simply, "I don't know yet," because speculating beyond what is written always comes from the evil one.

"But let your 'Yes' be 'Yes,' and your 'No,' 'No.' For whatever is more than these is from the evil one" (Matt. 5:37).

Playing guessing games with prophetic Scripture is like turning our minds into a playground for the devil. When the Scriptures are silent or unclear, we should be just as silent and unclear. When they are clear and explicit, we should be just as clear and explicit. Whether it's claiming to know who the restrainer is, who the two witnesses of Revelation are, claiming to understand the seventy-week prophecy of Daniel, the rebuilding of the Jewish temple, and a host of other such things, the reality is that many things are unclear.

When we let speculations muddy the water, the whole picture becomes muddied, making the clearly stated truths harder to recognize. Focus on getting what is clear about end-time truth right, and leave the speculation alone, because it's foolish and dangerous.

Jesus: The Master Teacher

Perhaps the reason the Lord warned us there would be a lot of deception over His coming was because of all the uncertainty surrounding it. Jesus told us that the Father is the only one who knows when this happens, so it's foolish to think we can figure it out. Jesus said He didn't know either, and we have no record of Him trying to figure it out.

Jesus was the greatest Bible teacher ever, so keep in mind how He taught about this: He gave us an overview first (Matt. 24:5–14); then He gave us the details (Matt. 24:15–31). The details cannot contradict the overview. He then helps us put it all together with illustrations or parables (Matt.

24:32–25:30) before finishing with an account of the judgment that happens when He comes (Matt. 25:31–46).

It's in the details section where people get into trouble, speculating on things like the abomination of desolation and the tribulation period. Don't let a few trees keep you from seeing the forest. While a jigsaw puzzle is put together one piece at a time, it is done so based on the big picture. Learning to agree with what Jesus said and staying within the boundaries of His overall end-times message will help to avoid much of the deception.

Jesus gave us the summary version first, so the right thing to do is make sure our theology fits within that summary. Anything true in His detailed account must fit into His summary account or He is contradicting Himself. It's really a brilliant way of teaching, because anything true and right about the sign of His coming has to fit inside His summary, while anything that doesn't fit has to be untrue and wrong. Rapture teachers will disagree, because their explanation of the details can't fit into the summary account.

To help avoid deception, follow Jesus's teaching as He taught it. Start with the summary, and use it as the guideline for understanding the details that follow. Doing that keeps us from heading off into a ditch. To help us stay on track, Jesus even gives us several parables after His detailed explanation. Our Lord really was the greatest Bible teacher of all, and He taught this Olivet Discourse in such a way as to keep us free from one of the worst deceptions of all—the deception over "signs" of His coming.

In His summary, there is no mention of cataclysmic events like the abomination of desolation, the sun being darkened, or the gathering of the elect from the four winds. In His summary, everything is much simpler, as Jesus tells us that the end comes when the gospel has been preached to every nation (Matt. 24:14). Although there is no specific answer given for the sign of His coming in His summary, the fact that He brought us to the end without doing so means we can safely reach the end without the need of such a sign. This is an important point for those determined to chase after signs. The truth is we don't need to figure out the signs—we just need to get the gospel out to every nation.

While rapture teachers freely admit there is no single Bible verse that proves their rapture, it's also true that their rapture doesn't even fit into the summary Jesus gave. Jesus said in Matthew 24:13 that if we endure until the end, we will be saved, and we can't endure if we get raptured seven years before the end.

Our hope should be in what Jesus promised, and not the speculations of men. Jesus warned us there would be many end-time deceivers among us, and they give themselves away when they would rather argue their position than accept the words of Jesus.

The Sign

The apostles asked Jesus, "What will be the sign of Your coming?" His answer will come as a surprise to those who follow today's popular prophecy experts. Their question was asked in Matthew 24:3, and the first time Jesus mentions it is right after the tribulation in verse 29. Even the real sign is in the wrong place for pre-trib theology!

"Then the sign of the Son of Man will appear in heaven, and then all the tribes of the earth will mourn, and they will see the Son of Man coming on the clouds of heaven with power and great glory" (Matt. 24:30).

The sign of His coming completely messes up pre-trib theology because that sign is seeing Jesus in the clouds when He comes *after* the tribulation. What Jesus said is far more relevant than all the speculations over a rebuilt temple, and He said *the* real sign is seeing Him coming on the clouds.

His answer fits perfectly within the summary He gave us, and it fits perfectly with no man knowing the day nor the hour. It fits perfectly with having to watch for His return, and for it to be as surprising as lightning flashing across the sky. It fits perfectly with His coming being like a thief in the night, and fits perfectly with His parable of the virgins with oil in their lamp. When it comes to the sign of His coming, Jesus said that sign is seeing Him as He comes.

Father Knows Best

Jesus told His disciples that it wasn't for us to know times or seasons. He also told us that no one knows the day or the hour. So those trying to build a timeline based on understanding the times and seasons void too many Scriptures to be taken seriously. When it comes to His coming, there must be nothing to tip us off: no Antichrist, no temple, no warnings, period. Knowing the times and seasons about the end is the exclusive property of the Father. Jesus reaffirmed this element of surprise by comparing His coming to the flood in the days of Noah: "But as the days of Noah were, so also will the coming of the Son of Man be. For as in the days before the flood, they were eating and drinking, marrying and giving in marriage, until the day that Noah entered the ark, and did not know until the flood came and took them all away, so also will the coming of the Son of Man be" (Matt. 24:37–39).

Those looking for the real signs right before Jesus returns should look for people to be eating and drinking and marrying. In other words, it will be life as usual on planet earth, right up until He appears in the clouds. Thus, the so-called great tribulation some prophets try to worry us with doesn't even interrupt the eating, drinking, and marrying of the world.

This makes pre-trib teaching on the great tribulation questionable, at best. If the world won't be bothered enough by the great tribulation to postpone weddings or carousing, what does that tell us about pre-trib theology? Jesus said if we endure until the end, we will be saved, so the defining question is whether or not we really believe Him. I know I do.

CHAPTER 8

THE END OF THE AGE

Speculation or Revelation?

Now as He sat on the Mount of Olives, the disciples came to Him privately, saying, "Tell us, when will these things be? And what will be the sign of Your coming, and of the end of the age?"

—Matthew 24:3

The third part to the disciples' question had to do with the end of the age. With Jesus telling them that the kingdom of God was leaving Israel and their temple was being destroyed, they likely thought this had to do with the end of the age. Like many people today, they were intrigued by the future and wanted a better understanding of it.

As Jesus answered the disciples' question, please note that the only prophets He mentioned were all false prophets. End-time deception is such a problem that despite His warnings, the disciples continued to speculate on the future right up to His ascension! Their final question before Jesus left reveals they still hadn't corrected their wrong way of thinking. Because such thinking is still prevalent in the church today, the answer Jesus gave is helpful to those who are serious about walking in the truth.

His answer was quite enlightening: "It is not for you to know times or seasons which the Father has put in His own authority" (Acts 1:7). In other words, Jesus said asking about such things is wrong because only the Father knows the prophetic times and seasons. This means we should keep our curiosity in check and avoid the speculative teaching of those who make a living trying to interpret times and seasons. Yet despite Jesus's command against it, speculation on the end times and its seasons has become big business in the church. There always seems to be popular prophetic teachers speculating about moons or something else that promises to help us better understand God's end-time plan.

The reality is that the Father has reserved the knowledge of prophetic times and seasons for Himself. The knowledge of these things is His exclusive property. To insist on pursuing knowledge of these things will only lead to deception. God exists outside the realm of time and knows the future better than we know the past. Those among us who claim to be able to break apocalyptic codes or explain hidden mysteries in the Scriptures are likely getting their guidance from a religious spirit because the Holy Spirit would never show us things Jesus said weren't for us to know.

How is it that so many genuine Christians can buy into a series on blood moons and then move on to the next prophetic fascination without any concern of being misled? How do we explain that the prophets who promoted the four blood moons have never apologized, and still have huge followings? Jesus said "many" would be deceived, and I've already explained how the church has learned to tolerate religious spirits, so let's leave the predicting to the tarot-card readers who welcome the help of these different spirits.

What we should learn from all this is to accept that some things simply aren't for us to know—like times and seasons. Instead of trying to figure out the end times, we should expect the seasons of the end times to be no clearer than what we see when looking through an opaque window. That's why Scriptures tell us now we only see "in a mirror dimly, but then (when He comes) face to face" (I Cor. 13:12). We're only asking for trouble by following the teaching of those claiming to have a clearer view, and we should dismiss all prophetic insight that we cannot verify in the Bible. Accurate teachers bring the Word of God to life while false teachers move us away from God's truth by speculating beyond what is written.

"For I testify to everyone who hears the words of the prophecy of this book: if anyone adds to these things, God will add to him the plagues that are written in this book; and if anyone takes away from the words of the book of this prophecy, God shall take away his part from the Book of Life, from the holy city, and from the things which are written in this book" (Rev. 22:18–19).

It's not just wrong to try and figure out unclear end-time prophecy; it could be a punishable offense. When people add or subtract from prophetic Scripture, they are trying to know the very things Jesus said were not ours to know. Trying to know what isn't for us to know opens the door to deceptive spirits—so don't do it!

Although there are many examples of adding or subtracting to prophecy, one that's easy to notice is the claim that the church is raptured in Revelation 4:1. I challenge anyone to find anywhere in that verse that the church is mentioned or even hinted at. Revelation 4:1 only describes John being caught up, so inserting the church into the verse is adding to the prophecy just like the book of Revelation warns against.

"When He, the Spirit of truth, has come, He will guide you into all truth; for He will not speak on His own authority, but whatever He hears He will speak; and He will tell you things to come" (John 16:13).

Instead of adding or subtracting to prophecy, the way we are supposed to learn is to look to the Holy Spirit to teach us. He has been assigned to tell us things to come, but He isn't going to add or take away from the Word to do it. What He will do is bring more life to what Jesus said (John 14:26). To not seek out the leading of the Holy Spirit is to open the door to deceptive spirits.

God doesn't want to punish us for adding or taking away from the prophecy, but the harm done by changing His Word can be so detrimental to people's faith that those doing it willfully will be punished. Everything God says, including the punishment for adding and subtracting to the prophecy, were written for our benefit, so take advantage of it. Let's now take a look at how the pre-trib view sees the end of the age.

The End of the Age as a Fable

The pre-trib storyline starts with the church being raptured and us becoming immortal (I Cor. 15:54). They have us raptured and going to heaven for either seven years, or three and a half years, depending on which story you believe. While we're in heaven, we'll be celebrating the marriage supper of the Lamb, but here on planet earth, great worldwide tribulation will be taking place. During this tribulation period, the pre-trib view teaches that God resumes some plan He had with Israel that they tell us has been put on hold while the church is here.[17] They believe this despite Paul using the first

____

17 . Pentecost, *Things to Come*, 201.

three chapters of Ephesians to explain that the church was always God's eternal purpose for both Jew and Gentile.

This means that rapture teachers have the church in heaven celebrating for seven years, while God is pouring out His wrath on the rest of the world—including His chosen people, Israel. This may be why some pre-trib pastors give greater support relocating Jews to Israel than to evangelizing them. But the reality is that any so-called love for Israel that doesn't include evangelism is disrespectful to Christ.

After all the bad stuff in the middle of the book of Revelation happens, the seven years of tribulation are complete, and Christ bursts through the clouds and returns in His Second Coming to begin His thousand-year reign known as the millennium. Pre-trib experts argue for this; they just cannot prove any of it from the Scriptures.

There is no Bible verse that clearly tells us this tribulation lasts seven years, nor is there a verse telling us the church is removed before it starts. One must add or take away from prophecy to have such knowledge of the times and seasons, and isn't it better to say, "I don't know because it isn't clear to me," than to be guilty of altering the Word? If we could know the times and seasons, then the coming of the Lord wouldn't be a surprise, and Jesus would be a liar.

It's true that the word "church" is absent from Revelation chapters 4–21, but so what! The book of Romans doesn't mention the word "church" until the last chapter, and no one is claiming its first fifteen chapters aren't for the church. The book of Galatians only mentions the word "church" in the first chapter, but no one questions whether the rest of the book is for the church. The absence of the word "church" in the middle chapters of Revelation only proves that the word "church" isn't there.

The word "saint" is mentioned plenty of times in the middle of the book of Revelation, and in the New Testament, a living "saint" is always a Christian (Eph. I:I; Phil. I:I; Col. I:2). When it comes to the book of Revelation, rapture teachers are inconsistent in their definition of "saint." They tell us the "saints" at the marriage supper of the Lamb (Rev. 19:7–9) are the church, but then tell us the "saints" in the tribulation are not. Picking and choosing like this from the same book of the Bible is yet another example of adding and taking away from the prophecy.

Ephesians I:22–23 tells us that the church is the fullness of Christ. If your glass is already full of iced tea, there's no room for lemonade. Since the church fills Christ, He's already full and has no room for another people called Israel. He only has one body, so Jews who want their inheritance need to trust Christ now in this age.

When pre-trib theology redefines a saint as someone outside the church, they do so without scriptural justification. They also put themselves at odds with what the church believed at the time the book of Revelation was written. Their pre-trib story becomes even more imaginative when they speak of their millennium as a literal thousand-year period.

The Millennium

This topic may be one of the most misunderstood end-time topics of all. Some pre-trib experts claim there is more scriptural proof of the millennium than any other prophetic topic,[18] but that is a matter of subjective interpretation. Jesus never mentioned the millennium in Matthew, chapter 24—or anywhere else, for that matter—and the epistle writer Paul never mentioned it anywhere either. In fact, the only place this thousand-year

---

18 . Pentecost, *Things to Come*, 476; Mark Hitchcock, *The End: A Complete Overview of Bible Prophecy and the End of Days* (Carol Stream, IL: Tyndale Momentum, 2012), 400.

period is specifically named is in Revelation, chapter 20, so it is wise not to make more of it than the Scriptures do.

If it was important for disciples to understand, then why didn't Jesus discuss it? Also, why didn't the early church mention the millennium in one of their creeds? Despite this quietness of the Scriptures, the pre-trib camp places such significance upon belief that the millennium is a literal future thousand-year reign of Christ that some of them are leery of even fellowshipping with those of us who dare to question this. Despite their insistence on millennial literalness, many of them don't know how ridiculously this must play out.

During the pre-trib version of the millennium, we, the immortal saints, are supposed to coexist for a thousand years with mortals who still reproduce and die.[19] When the thousand years are up, Satan is released to deceive them to battle against us (Rev. 20:7–9). But if we've become immortal, why would Satan even bother with such an attack? Imagine a deceived mortal trying to beat an immortal saint to death with a club. If this sounds imaginary and far-fetched, it's because that's what pre-trib teaching really is—far-fetched and imaginary. There is no evidence to support mortals and immortals living together like this. Rather than their version representing what is written in the prophecy, this is just another example of human error when men add to God's Word.

---

19 . John F. Walvoord, *The Rapture Question* (Grand Rapids, MI: Zondervan, 1979), 86.

Rightly Dividing the Word

*Be diligent to present yourself approved to God, a worker who does not
need to be ashamed, rightly dividing the word of truth.*

—2 Timothy 2:15

Talking about rightly dividing the Word doesn't qualify us to do it any
more than talking about gallbladder surgery qualifies us to perform that
operation. To rightly divide means to cut straight and true, like dissecting
or performing surgery. The work of a skillful surgeon is a good analogy
but with one important distinction—one is cutting physically, while the
other is cutting spiritually. Since there is a right way to divide the Word,
that means there is also a wrong way. So how do we know the right way? Is
it right because we say it's right, and is it wrong because we say it's wrong? Is
it right when it feels right, or wrong when it feels wrong? Whose judgment
do we rely upon to make the cuts?

It is easy to forget that we are called to trust in the Lord with all of
our heart, and to not lean on our own understanding. Forgetting this truth
is one reason intelligent and loving Christians can remain in disagreement
over truth. We must start with the premise that it's not up to us to decide
truth, it's up to us to recognize what God has decided.

We have already shown that this whole notion of us "deciding" what
is right and what is wrong was passed down from the garden. When God
created all things, He placed everything in its proper place, including right
and wrong. Mankind's sin was in taking it upon ourselves to be like God
and thinking we had the power to decide right from wrong.

When Jesus came on the scene, He came as the truth (John 14:6), and
when He left, He sent the Holy Spirit to guide us into all truth (John
15:26, 16:13). Why is this important? For one thing, He teaches us to deny

ourselves—that is to quit deciding right and wrong for ourselves. We don't decide the truth, God does. The Scriptures reveal His truth, and our role is to cooperate so the Holy Spirit can teach it to us. Truth has a name, and that name is Jesus Christ, so the Holy Spirit will always point us to Him. The only way to rightly divide is to divide so Jesus is always Lord of the Word. It also means we bow to whatever Jesus said. He said He was coming again, so we should accept that as the truth. Jesus also told His closest disciples that he who endures to the end shall be saved, so we should also accept that as the truth.

Genres

It's important to point out how the prophetic differs from the other genres. Other genres like the historical, poetic, and didactic Scripture should be interpreted differently. Historical Scriptures tell us what has happened; didactic Scriptures teach us what to believe, and how to live; while poetic Scriptures touch the emotions and inspire us to live for God. Prophetic Scriptures differ because they pertain to the unknown future, rather than to the known present or known past. This difference might seem obvious, but it requires us to treat prophetic Scripture differently.

People invite deception about the prophetic Scripture when they try to better understand the future than God has revealed. It's that gray area of uncertainty where deception takes place. Our focus should be on serving God and watching His Words come to pass, not trying to interpret prophecy. We should rejoice knowing that God our Father is so awesome that He can even give away His plan in a prophecy, and the enemy will still not see it coming nor be able to stop it. Prophetic Scriptures teach us to be ready and sober-minded because while we know it will come to pass, we don't know how. We are told enough to recognize a prophecy after it comes to pass, but generally not enough to recognize it before it happens.

Trying to understand prophetic Scripture ahead of it happening is like trying to describe what we see through an opaque window. Arguing for a literal interpretation of a prophecy—especially the visions in the book of Revelation—is like arguing that an abstract or surrealistic painting is realistic. God is the author of His Word, and He is the only one capable of rightly dividing it. To prove this, we will look at two biblical examples.

A Tale of Two Interpretations

To show how difficult it is to rightly divide the prophetic Word, let's take a look at two New Testament examples: First, a prophetic Scripture, and then, a prophetic vision. Let's begin with the master, our Lord Jesus Christ, and see how He handled a prophetic Scripture in Luke 4:17–20.

In this chapter of Luke, we read of Jesus being given the book of Isaiah and opening it to read a prophecy about Himself. He read Isaiah 61:1, and half of the next verse before stopping in midsentence. He then shut the book, and declared that what He'd just read was fulfilled that day. Let's look at the part of the prophecy He read, and then the part that He didn't read:

"The Spirit of the Lord God is upon Me, because the Lord has anointed Me to preach good tidings to the poor; He has sent Me to heal the brokenhearted, to proclaim liberty to the captives, and the opening of the prison to those who are bound; to proclaim the acceptable year of the Lord" (Isa. 61:1–2a).

It was as that point Jesus shut the book. Here is the rest of that verse: "And the day of vengeance of our God; to comfort all who mourn" (Isa. 61:2b).

Even though it starts with the word "and," Jesus shut the book before mentioning the day of vengeance. Would you or I have known to do that? Most prophecy experts and pastors would have thought the whole verse was the same prophecy. If they were there, they might have accused Him of misquoting the Scripture and wrongly dividing it. But Jesus was doing much more, because He was giving us a very important lesson regarding prophetic Scripture. It shouldn't come as a surprise that the religious people of Jesus's day didn't accept His teaching. They were more concerned about how He knew certain things. He told them His doctrine came from God (John 7:16), and that's always the right way God's Word is divided.

Unless we can say, as Jesus did, that God has shown us the truth, we really don't have God breathing life into our answer. There are too many divisions in the church involving some very smart and influential people, and it isn't for us to pick who is and isn't hearing from God; we must learn to hear from God for ourselves. Jesus said His sheep know His voice and follow Him. If you know Him, then you should know His voice. We simply cannot decide how to rightly divide prophetic Scripture without God's direction, and He has chosen to share such things as He wills with each of us through the Holy Spirit.

If Jesus had never quoted from Isaiah, the prophecy experts today would likely claim that the entire prophecy has to do with "the day of vengeance of our God." But Jesus changed everything by saying only a part of the verse was fulfilled. It takes the Holy Spirit to rightly divide as Jesus did, and when He does, there is no mistaking it.

Our second example is Peter's vision, found in Acts 10:9–16. Here, we read of Peter going up on the housetop to pray, where he became hungry waiting for the food to be prepared. He falls into a trance, and sees heaven open up. An object like a great sheet full of all kinds of animals, birds, and bugs descends down to him, followed by a voice telling him to rise and eat. Peter says he cannot eat anything unclean, and the voice replies not to call common what God has cleansed. This happened three times.

Pre-trib experts like to claim they interpret prophecy more accurately because they take the most literal approach. But if Peter had interpreted his vision literally, he would have gone around promoting that we eat bacon, shrimp, lobster, cockroaches, worms, and spiders, but He never did. If Peter had used the literal pre-trib approach to interpreting visions, he would have missed the real meaning.

What Peter did instead is very helpful because he showed us the right way to interpret prophetic visions. First, he didn't try to decide what he could literalize and develop a belief based around that. Instead, he pondered its meaning before God. This is the real key to understanding visionary Scripture—looking to the One who gave the vision to also reveal its meaning.

With Peter's mind open and receptive to what God was trying to teach him, the Holy Spirit spoke to Peter to go with the men who would show up at the door and to doubt nothing (Acts 10:19–20). If Peter hadn't taken time to ponder the vision, then the Holy Spirit might not have gotten through to him. Then, if Peter hadn't obeyed and gone with those men, he might never have gotten the answer he sought. But Peter did hear from the Holy Spirit, and he went with the men to the home of a Gentile, where he received his answer about the vision: "Then he said to them, 'You know how unlawful it is for a Jewish man to keep company with or go to one of another nation. But *God has shown me* that I should not call any man common or unclean'" (Acts 10:28).

Jesus said His doctrine came from God, and Peter said, "God has shown me." The right way to understand prophetic Scriptures and prophetic visions is to grasp what God shows us. If a prophecy teacher cannot say with certainty "God has shown me what it means," then they should keep quiet. If we ask God to help us see a prophetic truth, and He still doesn't make it clear, then we should leave it alone because it's still not for us to know "times" or "seasons." If there is something there He wants us to see, He heard our prayer, and will show us. It is the Holy Spirit that guides us into all truth, so let's not try to go there without Him.

The God who gave Jesus and Peter their answers also gave me my answers on the rapture. Yes, I will be so bold as to say, "God has shown me," but that doesn't mean you should blindly accept what I say. Jesus said His sheep know His voice, so it is His voice that you and I are to follow.

As Peter had to adjust his thinking about Gentiles, I had to adjust my thinking about the rapture. Peter had to step out of his comfort zone, and so did I, and it was then that God gave us both the answer. The best advice I can give you is to point you back to God and the Scriptures for answers. I asked and expected to know about the rapture according to John 16:13, and His voice of truth didn't disappoint. He first had to show me that my preconceived ideas had limited Him to answer me within pre-trib thinking, but once I took that restriction off Him, He was clear to show me.

John the revelator never wrote a commentary on the book of Revelation, but he did warn us against adding or taking away from the prophecy. When pre-trib teachers insist on a literal millennium with immortals living alongside mortals for a thousand years, they need to prove that "God has shown" them this. Any truth God shows about prophecy cannot be contradicted by the Scriptures, and it's easy to find Scripture that contradicts pre-trib.

The End of the Age: Really, This Time

When the disciples enquired about the end of the age, it was the "end" they wanted answers about. Rather than an elaborate, drawn-out story built to support a literal millennial viewpoint, Jesus gave a quick and easy answer: "And this gospel of the kingdom will be preached in all the world as a witness to all the nations and then the end will come" (Matt. 24:14).

According to Jesus, the end comes when the gospel has been preached to all nations, so we don't need a more complicated storyline than this. The gospel may have started with the lost sheep of Israel, but Jesus also had sheep from a different fold (John 10:16) because the gospel was always intended for all people. The Jewish church was so blind to Gentile inclusion that despite being filled with the Holy Spirit on the day of Pentecost, other than Philip's trip to Samaria, there is no record they evangelized Gentiles until Peter's vision of the unclean food eight years later. And Peter was called on the carpet for doing so (Acts 11:2–18).

The mystery of including Gentiles dated back to God telling Abram that in him all the families of the earth will be blessed (Gen. 12:3). This inclusive truth was always there in the Scriptures, hidden right in front of them. That's why interpreting prophecy is difficult—because unless the Lord opens our eyes, we might not see it, even when it's right in front of us. Failing to recognize prophetic fulfillment is to be expected because the Scriptures tell us it's like figuring out what we see in a dimly lit mirror.

"For now we see in a mirror, dimly, but then face to face" (1 Cor. 13:12).

The disciples heard Jesus declare earlier that the kingdom of God will be moving from Israel to another people (Matt. 21:43), but they didn't know that those people would be the multinational church. They couldn't see it! Before ascending to the Father, Jesus repeated their mission statement that the church is to carry out right up to the end: "Go therefore and make disciples of *all the nations*, baptizing them in the name of the Father and of the Son and of the Holy Spirit, teaching them to observe all things that I have commanded you; and lo, I am with you always, even *to the end of the age*" (Matt. 28:19–20).

Despite saying "all the nations" directly to them, they still missed it! Jesus also explained the end another way in Matthew 13:39, declaring that "the harvest is the end of the age." According to our Lord, the end happens after the church has made disciples from all nations because then it's harvest time. It's as simple as sowing seed and reaping a harvest or, as Paul wrote, "the simplicity that is in Christ" (2 Cor. 11:3).

The simplicity of God's plan is all around us, and speaks to us from creation every year. Every year, seeds bring forth new life and produce fruit for harvest; then winter kills them off until a resurrection of life happens again the following spring. It's easy to miss, just like the early Jewish church missed including Gentiles.

Beware of complicated stories that are not clear in the Scriptures. Here's what we know about the millennium: (1) Satan is bound, and cannot deceive as he did before this millennium; and (2) the only ones we are told who reign with Christ for the thousand years are in the "first resurrection" after rejecting the mark of the beast (Rev. 20:4–5). Reconciling these two points about the millennium without compromising either of them seems to be the key, and yet doing so proves the difficulty of grasping the meaning of prophetic visions unless God reveals it to us.

One thing we can do is eliminate the pre-trib rapture, because any claim of a resurrection earlier than this one in Revelation 20:4–6 takes away from the claim of "first resurrection" in this prophecy. None of us wants to be guilty of doing that. As we look at the next chapter, let's trust the Holy Spirit to make the Word of God even clearer to us.

CHAPTER 9

A CLOSER LOOK AT THE RAPTURE

Learning to Think Right

That you may learn in us not to think beyond what is written.
—I Corinthians 4:6

Learning not to think beyond what is written is a very different way of thinking than most are accustomed to. Both our thinking and the way we process thoughts must be changed, and it takes discipline on our part to effect those changes. It's such a drastic change that the Bible speaks of it as renewing the mind (Rom. 12:2), and it's necessary to prove the will of God.

This means we will only prove end-time truth when we do not allow our thoughts to wander beyond what is written in the Scriptures. Doing this requires taking every end-time thought captive to the obedience of Christ (2 Cor. 10:5). The Scriptures also say it this way: "Trust in the Lord with all your heart and lean not on your own understanding" (Prov. 3:5). We must learn to yield the right of way to God's Word on everything we believe. We must learn to replace our own ideas and feelings with what God says.

The world encourages us to decide things for ourselves while the Scriptures encourage us to believe what is written and obey it. Being a Christian is not a democracy where we get to choose the brand of Christianity we like best. Being a Christian means giving the Word of God first place in our lives; it means taking up our cross and following Jesus. It means knowing His voice and following Him.

Until we learn to make God's Word the determining factor in our thinking, our doctrine will be limited by what we decide is right, and that's just another way of saying we are still carnal-minded. Although it is subtle, it's this independent thinking that contributes to the vast doctrinal differences we see in the church. Pre-trib scholar Hilton Sutton spoke the truth when he said there isn't one verse of Scripture that proves the rapture, but the fact that it didn't change his mind shows just how influential our own minds can be.

Like so many other Christians, I once thought the rapture was scriptural. While I cannot speak for others, for me it was like seeing a mirage on the road and being convinced I saw water. To get to the truth, I had to take a closer look, and when I did, the mirage disappeared. This is the same thing we must do with the rapture; we must look close enough at the Scriptures for its truth to reveal itself, and when we do, this rapture will disappear.

I believed in the rapture not because I could prove it in the Scriptures, but because most of my favorite teachers believed in it. I believed in it because I *believed* it was in the Scriptures, even though I couldn't find it. I thought I was thinking right, and never suspected I was being misled by my own thinking. Instead of bringing every thought into captivity to the obedience of Christ (2 Cor. 10:5), my thoughts had taken me captive. I was only able to prove God's will on the rapture after admitting that my thinking might be wrong.

Why do so many honestly think there is Scripture to prove the rapture? In my case, it was a matter of not taking my thoughts captive and confusing the whisperings of a religious spirit as authoritative. Although this might sound foreign to some, the Bible teaches us that spirits are at work trying to trick us about end-time doctrine: "Now, brethren, concerning the coming of our Lord Jesus Christ and our gathering together to Him, we ask you, not to be soon shaken in mind or troubled, either *by spirit* or by word or letter, as if from us, as though the day of Christ had come" (2 Thess. 2:1–2).

If the pre-trib rapture were true, we would be able to find Bible verses to prove at least one of its two points that distinguish it from all other end-time views: (1) proof that the rapture occurs before the tribulation, or (2) proof that Jesus takes us to heaven when He meets us in the air. But since there isn't such a Scripture for either point, we should conclude that the Holy Spirit isn't teaching it. One of the best ways to expose a lie is to shine the light of God's Word directly on it. In these last few chapters, let's shine that light on some of the popular pre-trib talking points, starting with 1 Thessalonians 4:16–17.

Is the Rapture in 1 Thessalonians, Chapter 4?

For the Lord Himself will descend from heaven with a shout, with the voice of an archangel, and with the trumpet of God. And the dead in Christ will rise first. Then we who are alive and remain shall be caught up together with them in the clouds to meet the Lord in the air. And thus we shall always be with the Lord.

—1 Thessalonians 4:16-17

It's no secret that many pre-tribulation teachers refer to this text in I Thessalonians, chapter 4 as the greatest evidence of the rapture. But do these Scriptures really help their case? I used to think so, but now I know they don't. Let me explain.

First, claiming these verses prove the rapture is misleading because they don't tell us where we go after meeting the Lord in the air. We aren't told whether we change direction or if the Lord does. To decide that the Lord changes direction and whisks us back to heaven cannot be made by these Scriptures but must involve thinking beyond what is written. As previously shown, such additions to the Word are wrong.

A good illustration of the subtlety of this wrong thinking is found in the *MacArthur Reference Bible* comment on I Thessalonians 4:17. The author refers to the Greek word *harpazo*, which means "to seize, catch up, or snatch away." The author wants us to believe this is proof that this verse is speaking of us being raptured to heaven. But this is misleading, because every single time the word harpazo is used (thirteen times),[20] it tells us the destination for the "snatching away."

For example, the word is used in Acts 8:39–40, where the Spirit "caught" Philip away to the town of Azotus. Thus, the "harpazo" was to Azotus. In I Thessalonians 4:17, it also tells us where we are caught up to, and it isn't heaven—it's the clouds. It is scriptural to believe we are caught up to the clouds but unscriptural to assume we go from there to heaven. To suppose we go to heaven requires adding that assumption to the Scriptures, and as we learned from the garden of Eden, "harmlessly" adding to God's Word leads to deception.

---

20 . *Harpazo* is also found in Matthew II:I2, I2:29, I3:I9; John 6:I5, I0:I2, 28-29; Acts 8:39; 2 Corinthians I2:2, 4; Jude I:23; and Revelation I2:5.

When we meet the Lord in the air, someone must change direction, but rather than letting our thoughts decide this, let's take a closer look at the context and let the Scriptures tell us what is really going on here:

> But I do not want you to be ignorant, brethren, concerning those who have fallen asleep, lest you sorrow as others who have no hope. For if we believe that Jesus died and rose again, even so God will bring with Him those who fall asleep in Jesus. For this we say to you by the word of the Lord, that we who are alive and remain until the coming of the Lord will by no means precede those who are asleep. For the Lord Himself will descend from heaven with a shout, with the voice of an archangel, and with the trumpet of God. And the dead in Christ will rise first. Then we who are alive and remain shall be caught up together with them in the clouds to meet the Lord in the air. And thus we shall always be with the Lord. Therefore comfort one another with these words (1 Thess. 4:13–18).

To get the proper context, we need to include all the above verses. Verses 13 and 18 bring the other verses together like two slices of bread bring bacon, lettuce, and tomato together into a BLT sandwich. Without including verses 13 and 18, we miss the value and balance they bring to the context. Verse thirteen lets us know the subject is about their ignorance regarding those who die in Christ before He returns. Verse eighteen speaks of the comfort believers have when they are no longer ignorant about this.

There is no evidence that the Thessalonian church ever heard of a rapture before or after 1 Thessalonians was written, but there is plenty of evidence that they believed in the resurrection of the dead (Acts 4:2) and the coming of the Lord (Acts 1:11, 2:20). This is an important point because it tells us what the church knew and what they didn't know. There is no evidence they had concerns about a rapture because there is no proof they had ever heard of it. Their concerns were with what happened to those who died in Christ prior to the resurrection of the dead and the coming of the Lord. That's what Paul was clearing up for them.

Here's something Jesus said that might have spurred their questions: "Do not marvel at this; for the hour is coming in which all who are in the graves will hear His voice and come forth—those who have done good, to the resurrection of life, and those who have done evil, to the resurrection of condemnation" (John 5:28–29).

Even though John's gospel hadn't been written yet, Jesus's words were being passed around by word of mouth. They heard that Jesus had gone to the cross, they heard He had been resurrected, and they heard that He promised to return and resurrect the dead. The whole gospel is based on these great truths!

Unbelievers, on the other hand, will be resurrected to condemnation. Verse 13 in I Thessalonians, chapter 4 tells us when it comes to people who die in Christ, we are to sorrow differently than the world does. We have a hope that the world doesn't have. There is no hope apart from Christ, but being in Christ gives us great hope! Verse 14 then confirms that the church believed in the resurrection of Jesus. The power of the gospel is in the resurrection, and they had questions about how His return was connected to the resurrection of the dead. Questions like: What will happen to the souls of those who die before the resurrection? Or if their souls went to be with Christ, then what happens to them at the resurrection? Maybe they asked what happens during the resurrection to those still alive when Jesus returns. These were serious believers with legitimate questions about doctrine, and Paul was answering them.

If Paul was introducing the rapture, as pre-trib teachers assert, it would be a different resurrection than the one Jesus spoke of. If Paul had introduced a new doctrine, it would have led to new questions. But there is no evidence of this or of Paul ever differentiating a rapture from the Second Coming. There is also no evidence of him writing or saying that the resurrection of the church occurs much earlier than the general resurrection. In fact, we know Paul didn't believe in a separate rapture because of what he told Felix the governor several years after writing chapter 4 of I Thessalonians: "I have hope in God, which they themselves also accept, that there will be a resurrection of the dead, both of the just and the unjust" (Acts 24:15).

If Paul believed that a rapture happens seven years before the general resurrection, then he should have told Felix about it. But he only told him about the same resurrection of the just and the unjust that Jesus spoke of. Paul knew that good doctrine was based on agreeing with Jesus, and that's what he did with the resurrection. Paul was so committed to this practice that he told Timothy that anyone who didn't believe what Jesus said was proud and obsessed with disputes (I Tim. 6:3–4). In I Thessalonians, chapter 4, Paul wasn't introducing another resurrection; he was clarifying what happens to the saints during it.

Pre-trib teaching tries to convince us there is another earlier resurrection, which is something neither Jesus nor Paul said. Paul agreed with Jesus and believed the resurrection was for both the just and the unjust, and while he never hoped to be raptured, he did hope to be resurrected!

"If by any means, I may attain to the resurrection from the dead" (Phil. 3:11).

Verse 14 in I Thessalonians, chapter 4 tells us that "God will bring with Him those who sleep in Christ." So, yes, those who die do go to heaven, but they won't be left behind when Jesus returns because He brings them back with Him.

The concept of a rapture doesn't even make sense; why would Jesus bring them down to the clouds from heaven if in the same twinkling of an eye, He brings them right back? If this were a rapture, it would make more sense for them to just wait in heaven during that brief instance. But I Thessalonians 4:14 makes the point that God brings the departed saints back with Jesus because something more important than the rapture is going on; He's coming again, as promised, and that means it's resurrection time!

Pre-trib believes that all the events of the rapture happen in the twinkling of an eye. Yet why would Paul give us all those details in I Thessalonians 4 if it happens so quickly that no one would have time to notice any of them? Questions like this reveal the foolishness of insisting that Jesus turns around in mid-air. It's prideful to reject the possibility that we turn around in the air instead of Jesus. It makes much more sense for Jesus to bring saints from heaven with Him if He is actually returning back to earth. A trumpet sound and a procession of people make more sense if Christ is returning triumphantly!

Jesus said when He comes in His glory that all the nations will be gathered before Him. It is at that time when He separates the sheep from the goats, and gives the sheep their reward (Matt. 25:31–34). In chapter 4 of I Thessalonians, verses 16–17 have to do with the same resurrection of the dead because it's the only one the church knew about. They knew nothing of us vanishing in a rapture that many in our day are zealous to defend. Verse 15 comes right out and calls this "the coming of the Lord." This tells us in the clearest language possible that Jesus is coming back to the earth just as He promised! Jesus never promised to come again and again, and I Thessalonians 4:15 calls this "the" coming of the Lord. This is about Jesus keeping His promise.

We really cannot even call the rapture "a coming" because during the rapture, Jesus doesn't really come. He only meets us in the clouds as we are leaving for heaven, and it happens so quickly and secretively that the only thing people notice is us missing.

The popular book-series-turned-movie *Left Behind* gives us a vivid picture of what pre-tribulation teachers believe. In the movie, an elderly woman wakes from sleep on an airplane flight and notices her husband missing from his seat. She asks the person sitting nearby if he has seen her missing husband. Her husband's clothes are still lying on his seat, so she's worried he walked off somewhere naked. That's what pre-trib leads us to believe. I also watched a few minutes of another rapture movie, and in this one there is a flash in the sky (Matt. 24:27), followed by clothing dropping from the clouds as a helicopter crashes into the roof of a building. This disappearing act is what the pre-trib movement teaches will happen during the rapture, but there are no Scriptures to prove any of this.

With God giving us: (1) the shout, (2) the trumpet, (3) the dead rising first, and (4) Jesus coming in the clouds, it is very suspicious of pre-trib teaching to make all these things vanish in their secret rapture. Although pre-trib teaching imagines the shout in verse 16 is not heard by those of the world, Jesus said an hour is coming when "all" in the grave will hear His voice (John 5:28). If believers were raptured before the hour Jesus spoke of, then He misspoke about "all" hearing Him. Jesus didn't lie; I Thessalonians 4:16 confirms what He said in the context of the questions these believers had.

There is no scriptural proof that only the church hears the shout in I Thessalonians 4:16. What's the use of having a shout if no one hears it? Shouting is loud, and this shout is from heaven and loud enough to wake all the dead. Unless proven otherwise, expect this shout to be heard by everyone in the grave, just as Jesus said it would.

What about the trumpet of verse 16; are we to believe that no one hears that either? Trumpets mark significant events in the Bible, and Jesus said that when He comes on the clouds, there will be a great sound of a trumpet (Matt. 24:30–31). Paul confirms what Jesus said to His sheep in I Thessalonians 4:16. To believe the shout and the trumpet are somehow unheard by the world requires us to think and believe beyond what is written.

The Thessalonian church were Christians, so their faith was in Christ. Jesus was their savior, not Paul, so they were interested in what Jesus had to say. If Paul were introducing something new like a rapture, he would have to explain to them why what Jesus taught about His coming and the resurrection didn't apply to them. Pre-trib teachers may claim what Jesus said was for Jewish Israel, but Paul never did because he wasn't introducing a new doctrine.

Where is the scriptural proof of a rapture meeting with Jesus in the clouds where He is invisible to the world? There isn't one! Matthew 24:30 tells us, "And they shall see the Son of man coming in the clouds"; Revelation 1:7 says, "Behold, He is coming with clouds, and *every eye* will see Him." The real truth is established from the mouth of two or three witnesses (Matt. 18:16; 2 Cor. 13:1). Every other place in the Scriptures where Jesus comes in the clouds, the people see Him (Matt. 24:30, 26:64; Mark 13:26, 14:62; Rev. 1:7). It's only the rapture teaching that makes His appearance invisible. Pre-trib teachers must prove that no one left behind sees or hears the details of the account in I Thessalonians, chapter 4.

Pre-trib also teaches that the rapture happens in the twinkling of an eye. But their so-called proof text requires adding to the text as well because it is really just a reference to how quickly we are changed.[21] The evidence of Scripture is that when Jesus comes on the clouds, He is seen. The only way to justify a secret escape is by holding on to thoughts and beliefs that cannot be verified by the Scriptures.

---

21 . I Corinthians 15:51–52 notice "We shall all be changed in a moment, in a twinkling of an eye."

The text in I Thessalonians 4:15 tells us plainly that this is *"the* coming of the Lord," so it isn't a practice run—it's the real thing, and He is coming! Verse 17 tells us our part is to "meet" the Lord in the air, not vanish into heaven. He does the "coming," and we do the "meeting." It becomes clearer once we stop confusing who is coming with who is meeting. He's not meeting us as we leave—we are meeting Him as He comes.

If I promise to come preach at your church and you agree to meet me at the airport, who changes directions at the airport? Jesus promised to come, and if we are alive, we meet Him in the air when He does. If we die before He comes, then we shall come back with Him, but either way, He is still coming! Instead of making the details of I Thessalonians 4:16–17 vanish in the twinkling of an eye, let's compare its details with similar scriptural accounts to help confirm what the Scriptures really say.

A Tale of Four Trumpets

There are four trumpet accounts in the New Testament that we should compare. Those four are found in: I Thessalonians 4:16–17; I Corinthians 15:51–54; Matthew 24:30–31; and Revelation 11:15–18.

Pre-trib teachers agree that the first two accounts—in I Thessalonians, chapter 4, and I Corinthians, chapter 15—both speak of the rapture but not the Second Coming. Pre-trib teachers also insist that the other two accounts—Matthew 24:30–31 and Revelation 11:15–18 —speak of the Second Coming but not the rapture. I have put together a helpful table so you can make side-by-side comparisons and decide for yourself:

I Thess. 4:16–17	I Cor. 15:51–54	Matt. 24:30–31	Rev. 11:15–18	Similarity
X	X	X	X	Trumpet
	X		X	Last trumpet
X	X	X	X	Dead raised/judged
X	X		X	Living changed
X		X	X	Angel(s)
X			X	Loud voice
	X		X	Death conquered/judged
	X		X	Rewards/immortality
X		X		Clouds
X		X	X	Lord descends/kingdom becomes His

If pre-trib teaching were right, we would expect the trumpet of I Thessalonians, chapter 4 to have the most in common with the trumpet of I Corinthians, chapter 15—but that's not the case. While the former has three things in common with the latter, it has five things in common with the trumpet in Matthew, chapter 24—and six things in common with the trumpet in Revelation, chapter 11. This means the trumpet of I Thessalonians, chapter 4 has twice as much in common with the trumpet of Revelation, chapter 11 as with the trumpet in I Corinthians, chapter 15. This clearly goes against the claim of the pre-trib argument. If they insist that the two accounts with the least in common describe the same event, then they cannot excuse the accounts with more in common just because they don't fit their theology. Honesty and humility should lead us to accept scriptural truth.

I wasn't kidding about gladly switching to pre-trib if there were scriptural proof to do so—there just isn't any! I've read books by pre-trib experts containing long lists meant to persuade me that the trumpet in chapter 11 of Revelation is different than the rapture trumpet of I Thessalonians, chapter 4, or I Corinthians, chapter 15, but I couldn't find a single shred of real evidence anywhere on those lists. Rather than pointing out the error in every item on those lists, I created the table so you can compare the facts and decide for yourself. By the way, did you notice that the account in Revelation, chapter 11 has twice as many similarities with I Corinthians, chapter 15 and I Thessalonians, chapter 4 as they have with each other?

Summary of I Thessalonians, Chapter 4

The evidence is overwhelming that one of the favorite Scripture references used by rapture teachers is really describing the coming of the Lord. There is no evidence that Jesus changes directions in the air, either in I Thessalonians, chapter 4, or anywhere else in the Bible. There is overwhelming evidence that Jesus is coming again as promised but no evidence that the shout or trumpet are only heard by Christians. There is also no evidence we go to heaven after meeting the Lord in the air. In other words, there is no evidence anywhere in the Bible to support a pre-trib rapture. Verse 15 in I Thessalonians, chapter 4 calls this the coming of the Lord, so if we say this isn't His coming, then we simply don't believe the Scriptures.

CHAPTER 10

A CLOSER LOOK: PART II

Let's now turn our attention to some of the favorite pre-trib arguments.

John, Chapter 14

In My Father's house are many mansions; if it were not so, I would have told you. I go to prepare a place for you. And if I go and prepare a place for you, I will come again and receive you to Myself; that where I am, there you may be also.

—John 14:2-3

Some pre-trib teachers claim these Scriptures describe Jesus rapturing us to heaven. But heaven isn't mentioned anywhere in these verses, so they must add the idea of heaven to the text to make that work. Adding to the Word *always* changes its meaning, and that is something we aren't supposed to do. What we are supposed to do is believe the Scriptures.

Some preachers think Jesus went to heaven to prepare a place for us, but if He hadn't gone to the cross, we couldn't go to heaven. Jesus didn't arrive in heaven, pull out His carpenter toolbox, and start building mansions. His work was done on the cross, and when He was finished there, he said, "It is finished."

Instead of changing God's Word, we should trust that everything we need to know can be found in the Scriptures. If we're willing to accept it, we find that Jesus tells us what is going on when He says, "I will come again." This isn't the language of someone taking us to heaven, this is the language of someone who is coming here. Jesus even restates this later in the chapter at John 14:28 when He says, "You have heard Me say to you, I am going away and coming back to you." He's not coming to take us away, He's coming back to be with us.

John 14:2–3 describes Jesus coming back as He promised. While He never says anything about coming to get us and take us to heaven, there are at least twelve other places where He said He will come again (Matt. 16:27; 24:27, 30, 37, 39; 25:31; 26:64; Mark 13:26, 36; 14:62; Luke 21:27; John 14:28). If we are believers, then we will believe the Lord.

Please look closely at the following text with me: "Now when He had spoken these things, while they watched, He was taken up, and a cloud received Him out of their sight. And while they looked steadfastly toward heaven as He went up, behold, two men stood by them in white apparel, who also said, 'Men of Galilee, why do you stand gazing up into heaven? This same Jesus, who was taken up from you into heaven, will so come in like manner as you saw Him go into heaven'" (Acts 1:9–11).

That day, the disciples saw what the coming of the Lord will look like. Simply reverse the direction, and we will know what to expect: He will leave heaven, travel in the clouds, and return back to planet earth. It's that simple because Jesus is coming again as promised!

Kept from the Hour of Trial

Another popular argument comes from the belief that being kept from the hour of trial means being raptured before the tribulation.[22]

"Because you have kept My command to persevere, I also will keep you from the hour of trial which shall come upon the whole world, to test those who dwell on the earth" (Rev. 3:10).

The book of Revelation was written to the seven churches in Asia, and many pre-trib advocates choose to identify with only one of those churches—the faithful church that's kept from the hour of trial. How did they decide that they are this church? Given the examples I've shown of them not agreeing with the Scriptures, what is the basis for them being faithful?

Despite their many shortcomings, let's play along and suppose that pre-trib teaching is right about Revelation 3:10. But let's do this only on one condition: that we limit ourselves to agreeing with what the verse really says, and not stray off to something it doesn't say. This means their argument must be made on the strength of God's Word alone and not the words of man. Doing this, we should be able to determine if Revelation 3:10 refers to the rapture. Let's take a look and see.

The Greek word for "keep" is used twice in Revelation 3:10, once interpreted as "kept," and the other as "keep." The verse tells us Jesus keeps these believers from the hour of trial because they kept His command to persevere or endure. Notice that they are kept because they persevere—not so they could avoid it.

When did Jesus tell them to do this? By cross-checking my concordance with the NKJV, I found only one place, and that was in Luke 21:19, where

____

22 . Hilton Sutton, *The Book of Revelation Revealed: An In-Depth Study on the Book of Revelation* (Tulsa, OK: Harrison House Inc., 2001), 64–67; Pentecost, *Things to Come*, 216.

the Greek word translated as "persevere" in Revelation 3:10, is translated as "patience." This patience or perseverance is for the time when others are being killed, betrayed, hated, and many falling away from the faith. By comparing the account of Luke 21:12-19 with Matt. 24:9–13, we see this is about persevering until the end. Thus, being kept from the hour of trial cannot mean escaping what they've already endured until the end. It means being kept from falling away from the faith.

Rapture teachers claim Jesus was speaking about Israel in Matthew, chapter 24, so according to their theology, the Philadelphia church was rewarded for keeping a command that wasn't even for them. Their logic doesn't hold up. This is the only account where Jesus gave such a command, and He gave it to His followers, and it had to do with our proper response to great tribulation. The reward of Revelation 3:10 comes from enduring tribulation, so it cannot refer to a rapture escape.

To further validate this, let's look at the text that follows Revelation 3:10: "Behold, I am coming quickly! Hold fast what you have, that no one may take your crown. He who overcomes, I will make him a pillar in the temple of My God, and he shall go out no more. I will write on him the name of My God and the name of the city of My God, the New Jerusalem, which comes down out of heaven from My God" (Rev. 3:11–12).

Right after promising to "keep" them because they persevered, the Lord tells them He is coming quickly. Notice that He doesn't say He is coming to rescue them to heaven, but that He is coming back and bringing New Jerusalem with Him. Would New Jerusalem come with Him if they were going to turn around in mid-air and return back to heaven? Of course not! We only read of New Jerusalem coming down from heaven but never of it going back, so let's not add to the Scriptures. If this were the rapture, then Jesus should have said He is going to rescue us quickly, but He didn't because it's not the rapture! We need to hold fast what we have to keep our crown, and that means enduring until the end.

"And they overcame him by the blood of the Lamb and by the word of their testimony, and they did not love their lives to the death" (Rev. 12:11).

Some who persevere will be rewarded by being kept from death and destruction until Jesus returns. Others will die for their faith. When Jesus returns, there will be believers here whose commitment to Him exceeds their fear of death, proving that they are part of the victorious overcoming church. Those expecting to be raptured might not have the resolve and determination to endure, but all are encouraged to put on the full armor of God (Eph. 6:10–13). Not only are there no Scriptures to support a rapture escape—Jesus actually prayed *against* it!

Jesus Prays Against the Rapture

I have given them Your Word; and the world has hated them because they are not of the world, just as I am not of the world. I do not pray that You should take them out of the world, but that You should keep them from the evil one . . . I do not pray for these alone, but also for those who will believe in Me through their word.

—John 17:14–15, 20

Before going to the cross, our Lord prayed for all His disciples. We know He included us because He prayed for those who believe through the preached word. If Jesus wanted us to be raptured, then He would have prayed for us to be taken out of the world, but instead, He prayed contrary to that. Instead of praying for our rapture, He prayed we be "kept" (there's that word again) from the evil one while remaining here. He was very specific about us not being "taken" out of this world.

John 17:20 says He was praying for all who will believe in Him through their word—so this was not just for those first disciples, but for the entire church! Jesus specifically prayed against the church being raptured, so shouldn't we believe Him?

God Won't Beat Up His Bride

A fellow Bible school student once told me his favorite reason for believing in the rapture came from a popular TV preacher who said something like, "The Lord will rapture us because He isn't going to beat up His bride before marrying her!" For those unfamiliar with this kind of argument, it has to do with the notion that being left behind during the tribulation equates to God beating up His people.

This argument is faulty on many levels: First, it comes from the same people who insist Israel are God's chosen people, yet they leave them behind to get beaten up during the tribulation. This means they have God beating up some of His people (Israel) but not us (the church). Second, this argument reminds us why it's important to understand the difference between tribulation and wrath. Tribulation comes from Satan against the Word, and wrath comes from God against the unbeliever. Verse 9 in 1 Thessalonians, chapter 5 teaches that saved people are always spared from God's wrath, even during times of great tribulation. Third, Isaiah 52:14 tells us Jesus was marred more than any man, so He was nearly beaten to death before being crucified for us. Does this mean God beat Him up before the wedding? And why is the church His bride instead of Israel? Finally, much of the church has already died, and their bodies have been fully decayed, so those bodies will be in worse shape than any beaten-up bodies.

Jesus Christ is Lord, and He said we rise to meet Him on the last day (John 6:44), so let's not water down what He said. In Matthew, chapter 16, Jesus began to tell His disciples that He must suffer many things and be killed, but Peter rebuked Jesus for saying this! Using the argument that God doesn't beat up His bride is like siding with Peter here, and Jesus responded to him with, "Get behind Me, Satan!" (Matt. 16:21–23). Let's now look at the state of the earth right before Jesus returns.

The Great Tribulation

But as the days of Noah were, so also will the coming of the Son of Man be . . . they were eating and drinking, marrying and giving in marriage, until the day that Noah entered the ark . . . so also will the coming of the Son of Man be.

—Matthew 24:37–39

Based on what we read in the book of Revelation, many Christians expect a future great tribulation to hit the earth that will be so bad they can't imagine God leaving them here to endure it. But here in Matthew, chapter 24, Jesus points out people will be marrying and giving in marriage right up to the time of His Second Coming. Did Jesus tell us the truth? If the events in the book of Revelation were literal, then no one would be carrying on normally, and people could calculate the day of Jesus's return based on when such things started. But Jesus also said no man knows the day, nor the hour, and that only makes sense if people will be carrying on as normal right up to His Second Coming.

So, what do we do with all the catastrophic things spoken of in the book of Revelation? The only thing we can do: We don't impose an interpretation that contradicts what Jesus said. Keep in mind that those images in Revelation were given in a vision, and visions, like Peter's in the book of Acts, can be symbolic. Good theology is based on the rock of our salvation, and that means building on Christ and what He taught us. We should trust that the visions of Revelation are true but accept the possibility that prophecy experts may not understand them as well as they let on.

We already discussed Peter's vision, and showed that he only understood the meaning of the vision after God showed it to him (Acts 10:28, 11:5–18) and it wasn't literal. So, let's not jump to literal conclusions about the imagery in Revelation because, like Peter's vision, it probably has more spiritual meaning than physical. There is no question that some bad stuff happens in Revelation, but we are on the winning team, and our salvation keeps us from God's wrath.

Take Jesus at His word that people will be marrying and giving in marriage right up until He returns. Take Him at His word that no one knows the day nor the hour, and quit following prophetic experts with their timelines for how it works out. Take Jesus at His word that we will be as surprised by His return as we would be by a thief in the night.

The safest thing to do with Scriptures describing visions is to believe them without adding or taking away from them. Even the basis for the so-called seven-year tribulation is based on interpreting a vision given to Daniel (Dan. 9:20–27). The reality is that arguments about the timeline for the seventy weeks in Daniel's prophecy of Daniel 9:24–27 are fruitless because every calendar is man-made and subject to error.[23] Right before Jesus ascended to the Father, He told us that times and seasons weren't for

---

23 . Rabbi Bentzion Kravitz, "Daniel 9: A True Biblical Interpretation," Jews for Judaism.org, accessed 07/2018, https://jewsforjudaism.org/knowledge/articles/daniel-9-a-true-biblical-interpretation. The article states there is no reliable source for the exact starting date for the prophecy used by many Christians.

us (His disciples) to know, so the right thing to do is to stay away from such unfruitful works.

We still see through a glass darkly, and speculation on these things only gets us into trouble. Stick with what Jesus said as literal, and let the prophetic reveal itself. The dangers associated with men trying to figure out the visionary and prophetic Scriptures are a big part of why Jesus said to take heed no one deceives us. Jesus won't deceive us, so let's stick with Him!

One Taken and One Left

Then two men will be in the field: one will be taken and the other left. Two women will be grinding at the mill: one will be taken and the other left.

—Matthew 24:40–41

Many people believe this is evidence of the rapture. But that cannot be the case because Jesus was comparing His coming with the days of Noah and the ark. At Noah's flood, it wasn't Noah who was taken away—it was the people outside the ark. The proof is in Matthew 24:39, where it says they "did not know until the flood came and took them all away." Noah knew the flood was coming and built the ark to prepare for it! Noah and his family were kept from the flood, not surprised and taken away by it. Instead of us being raptured, it's the unbelievers who are taken away.

In Matthew 13:40–41, Jesus verifies this by telling us it's the tares or sons of the wicked one who are gathered away to be burned. God created the earth for His people, so He isn't going to discard it, but will remake it for us to enjoy. Jesus shall return and be with us when the earth is made new. Jesus told us in Matthew 5:5 that the meek inherit the earth, and that inheritance is forever (Ps. 37:9-18).

I Thessalonians 1:10

Although I've never read of this verse being used as pre-trib proof, several of the pastors responding to my survey cited it as proof of the rapture, so let's look at it next: "And to wait for His Son from heaven, whom He raised from the dead, even Jesus who delivers us from the wrath to come" (I Thess. 1:10).

Would Paul speak of a benefit to a rapture that he never explained to this church, or was he reminding them of the power in the death and resurrection of Christ? We've already shown that both John 3:36 and I Thessalonians 5:9 contrast salvation with wrath, and since there is no Scripture to prove a rapture, the only right conclusion is he's reminding them of their great salvation. Verse 10 in I Thessalonians, chapter 1 tells us to wait for His Son from heaven because there is coming a day when Jesus will leave heaven to return here just like He promised. When He returns, it's time for the wrath to come as Revelation 11:17–18 tells us.

Seven Raptures

Another argument intended to justify the rapture of the church is the argument that there are seven raptures in the Bible.[24] Just because God translated Enoch, Elijah, and Jesus (in His ascension) doesn't justify a pre-trib rapture for the resurrection of the saints. As my mother used to say, "If Johnny jumped off a cliff, does that mean you should?" Even if God translated one person every year since the history of humanity, it still wouldn't justify that a rapture escape is God's plan for the church.

---

24 . Hilton Sutton, *Rapture: Get Right or Get Left* (Tulsa, OK: Harrison House, Inc., 1991), 9–35.

The only good argument to prove a rapture must come from the Scriptures. The Word of God alone decides such truths for us. The Scriptures tell us that *all* will rise at the coming of the Lord (I Thess. 4:15–17; John 5:28–29), when the last trumpet sounds (I Cor. 15:51–52), at the last day (John 6:40). There cannot be a rapture/resurrection several years before the Coming of the Lord. Stay with God's Word to avoid being misled. His Word doesn't say we get to leave for seven years or even three and a half years. What the Scriptures tell us clearly is that He is coming and He who endures until the end shall be saved (Matt. 24:13).

CHAPTER 11

LAST THINGS

Last Trumpet

Behold, I tell you a mystery: We shall not all sleep, but we shall all be changed—in a moment, in the twinkling of an eye, at the last trumpet. For the trumpet will sound, and the dead will be raised incorruptible, and we shall be changed.

—I Corinthians 15:51–52

During my thirty-plus years of studying the end times, I've noticed that many people believe the above mystery refers to the rapture. I've even heard pre-trib experts use the "twinkling of an eye" to explain how we vanish so quickly that the world won't hear the trumpet or see Jesus in the sky. But the Bible doesn't say that—it only tells us we are changed in the twinkling of an eye. This isn't about disappearing, it's about how quickly we are changed at the resurrection.

When we read these Scriptures in their context, we discover Paul was talking about the resurrection of the dead.[25] Verse 54 in I Corinthians, chapter 15 contains a direct quote from Isaiah 25:8, telling us that "death is being swallowed up in victory." This says nothing about vanishing to heaven because it is about the resurrection of the dead.

The trumpet will sound, and we will be changed. All the graves will be emptied once and for all as death is abolished forever. Jesus said this would happen (John 5:28–29), and Paul quoted an Old Testament prophecy to prove the consistency of God's Word. If sinners are not resurrected at this time, then both Isaiah and Paul lied about death being completely swallowed up in victory. If someone were to die in a tribulation after the last trumpet of I Corinthians, then death couldn't have been swallowed up in victory, and the Scriptures would be false. Paul agreed with the Old Testament and the words of Jesus. He also told us what we should know about Bible teachers who do not agree with the words of Jesus: "If anyone teaches otherwise and does not consent to wholesome words, even *the words of our Lord Jesus Christ,* and to the doctrine which accords with godliness, he is proud, knowing nothing, but is obsessed with disputes and arguments over words . . ." (I Tim. 6:3–4).

In addition to having to explain away the complete victory over death, perhaps a bigger problem pre-trib theologians have with the text of I Corinthians 15:52 is that it clearly tells us this trumpet is the "last" trumpet. The CEB version calls it "the final trumpet." Most people are usually not confused about the meaning of "last," and yet pre-trib teachers are convinced that seven trumpets will still sound after this final trumpet.

When it comes to this last trumpet, the word "last" in I Corinthians 15:52 is one of those battleground words that pre-trib teachers must forever

---

25 . See I Corinthians 15:20–58 for full context.

dispute.[26] For pre-trib teachers to concede this as the "last trumpet" equates to admitting that they are wrong. The Bible warns of such false teachers who are obsessed with disputes and arguments over words, and those redefining this last trumpet are a great example of that. Those who are committed to being scriptural will choose the plain meaning of Scripture over the misleading rapture teaching.

In I Corinthians 15:51, Paul speaks of a mystery regarding those alive at the resurrection when Christ returns. While the church knew about the resurrection of the dead, they were unclear about what happens to those still living when it happens. While rapture teachers insist the rapture happens many years before the Second Coming, Paul never even hinted at such a thing. Paul told us to consent to the words of Jesus, and that is what he did. He wrote about the same resurrection Jesus spoke of in order to help us better understand it.

God's Word would be misleading and confusing if there were seven trumpets of Revelation after this "last" trumpet of I Corinthians 15. If any trumpets come after the one that the Bible clearly says is the last trumpet, then God's Word is not true and God cannot be trusted. If we cannot trust God's Word, then we cannot trust anyone's word. Rather than explaining away the last trumpet as not being last, let's just agree with what the Holy Spirit had Paul write.

The Holy Spirit guides us into all truth, so He won't ever mislead us. The Bible says those obsessed with disputing what is written are the ones trying to mislead us. Think about that the next time a preacher refuses to accept the trumpet of I Corinthians 15:52 as the final one. Go back to my

---

26 . Pre-trib teaching is guilty of changing the last trumpet of I Corinthians 15:52; the last day of John 6:39–40; the falling away of 2 Thessalonians 2:3; the wrath of I Thessalonians 5:9; and the coming of the Lord in I Thessalonians 4:15.

table in chapter nine, and let the evidence speak for itself. The Scriptures will only make sense when the last trumpet happens on the last day.

Last Day

This is the will of the Father who sent Me, that of all He has given Me I should lose nothing, but should raise it up at the last day.

—John 6:39

Hopefully, by now you realize there is a lot of deception with the pre-tribulation rapture. For those willing to accept the truth, Jesus tells us very clearly that God's will is for all of us to be resurrected at the last day. And because it's the last day, as with the last trumpet, there cannot be any days with tribulation or death after this. Also, there can't be a rapture before this day because Jesus tells us that "all" the Father has given Him will be raised at that time. All means all, so all of us will be raised at that time and not before it.

"And this is the will of Him who sent Me, that everyone who sees the Son and believes in Him may have everlasting life; and I will raise him up at the *last day*" (John 6:40).

Pre-trib teachers try to convince us that Jesus was only referring to Jewish Israel.[27] We know that cannot be right because Jesus said this applied to "everyone who sees the Son and believes in Him." If we believe in Him as Lord and have eternal life, then He meant this for us as well. Jesus died for the sins of the whole world, so when He speaks of "everyone," don't believe those who limit the audience to Jewish Israel.

---

27 . Pentecost, *Things to Come*, 175.

Pre-trib teachers also change the meaning of the last day into a much longer period of time. This allows them to fit their rapture, seven years of tribulation, the Second Coming, and the millennium all into that last day! Wow, what happened to simply believing Jesus?

"No one can come to Me unless the Father who sent Me draws him; and I will raise him up at the *last day*" (John 6:44).

This is the third time our Lord tells us that He will raise us up at the last day. Anyone who the Father draws to Jesus gets raised at the last day, so He wasn't speaking of an Israel that rejects Him, but of a people that love Him—His church. God so loved the world He gave His only begotten Son that whosoever believes in Him will have everlasting life, and God will raise all of us at the last day.

"Whoever eats My flesh and drinks My blood has eternal life, and I will raise him up at the *last day*" (John 6:54).

This makes four times that Jesus said the resurrection occurs at the last day. While He said it slightly different each time, He always said it happens at the last day. This time, He tells us the last day resurrection applies to all who come to the communion table because of their trust in Him. Those who reject the words of Jesus do so to their own detriment, and those committed to following Him will choose His word over the words of any preacher, no matter who they are. Jesus said we are resurrected at the last day four different times, and if He wanted us to believe something different, He would have said so.

The problem with false teaching is that it doesn't honor Christ because it doesn't believe Him. Jesus warned us this would happen. He said deceivers would come in His name, and Paul told us they would disagree with the words of our Lord. He told us they would dispute and argue over such words, and I've just shown a doctrine that does that repeatedly.

I believe most pastors want the truth, and should be given the benefit of the doubt. Don't abandon a good pastor just because he may not know this truth yet. It is only when a pastor is adamant and insistent on teaching error that the Bible instructs us to withdraw from them (I Tim. 6:3–5). Following the real Jesus always costs something, and sometimes that means losing fellowship. The first disciples were shunned by the religious majority, and even Luther was shunned by the church of his day, so don't be surprised by churches that choose their end-time doctrine over biblical truth they don't agree with.

The End-Time Harvest

Allow me to paraphrase the parable of the wheat and the tares: "The kingdom of heaven is like a man who sowed good seed in his field. While men slept, his enemy sowed tares among the wheat. Both wheat and tare sprouted and produced crops. The owner's servants then offered to pull up the tares. The owner said no, because that would uproot the wheat." Then he said this: "Let both grow together until the harvest, and at the time of harvest I will say to the reapers, 'First gather together the tares and bind them in bundles to burn them, but gather the wheat into my barn'" (Matt. 13:30).

Here is how Jesus went on to explain the parable: "Therefore as the tares are gathered and burned in the fire, so it will be at the end of this age. The Son of Man will send out His angels, and they will gather out of His kingdom all things that offend, and those who practice lawlessness, and will cast them into the furnace of fire. There will be wailing and gnashing of teeth. Then the righteous will shine forth as the sun in the kingdom of their Father. He who has ears to hear, let him hear!" (Matt. 13:40–43).

We have already shown proof that an hour is coming when all who are in the graves will hear the voice of Jesus and come forth to a resurrection of life or condemnation (John 5:28–29). This parable of the wheat and tares should help us better understand the resurrection, but it only will when we have ears to hear the truth that Jesus keeps telling us! Keep in mind that Jesus said many of His own disciples would be deceived over the end times (Matt. 24:4–5).

The parable of the wheat and tares is much easier to understand than the heavenly vision in the book of Revelation. Jesus made it easy so those with ears to hear would understand how the end really plays out. The more complicated a story becomes, the easier it is to weave deception into it. While the words of Jesus are easy to prove from Scripture, the pre-trib model is complicated and cannot be proven. Jesus said, "He who has ears to hear, let him hear!" We can choose to believe Him, or choose not to. Either He spoke the truth in the parable, or He didn't.

Jesus spoke the same truth in John 5:28–29 about "all" coming forth from their graves. He even told us that some would come forth to a resurrection of life while others to a resurrection of condemnation. The resurrection is clearly for all people. Jesus also said in John 12:32 that He "will draw all people" to Himself, and the words "all people" only come alive if "all" are resurrected.

In Matthew, chapter 25, Jesus told us when He comes in His glory that "all" the nations will be gathered before Him. All the nations is another way of saying "all the people," and it makes perfect sense for Him to separate the sheep from the goats (Matt. 25:31–46) at that time. Everything fits and is much easier to understand when we just believe what Jesus said.

Earlier, we pointed out that it was the wicked ones who were taken away during Noah's day. When Jesus explains the great end-time harvest in Matthew, chapter 13, He tells us that these sons of the wicked one will not be taken away by water but taken to be burned in the fire. Revelation 11:18 describes this as a time of God's wrath and for judging the dead.

Revelation 1:7 describes Jesus's coming as being seen by every eye as all the tribes of the earth wail or mourn in grief. They will mourn in grief, because at that point, they only have an eternal fire to look forward to! Matthew 25:46 calls what awaits them everlasting punishment. For those who haven't turned to Christ, this will be the beginning of a horrible eternal fire. Eternity is a long time to be wrong. If you haven't already done so, please choose life in Christ now! Call upon the name of the Lord and be saved from yourself, your sin, and your everlasting punishment. His name is Jesus Christ, and He alone has conquered death and the grave.

Some argue that the parable is different from the rapture on the basis that in the parable the tares are raised first (Matt. 13:30), while at the rapture it's the dead in Christ raised first (1 Thess. 4:16). This is just a confusion about the contexts. Jesus was comparing the ungodly to the godly, while Paul was comparing the dead in Christ to the living in Christ. Jesus said that an hour was coming when "all" who are in the grave will hear His voice (John 5:28), so it comes down to whether or not we believe Him.

It is only when we trust what is written that everything fits perfectly: We have the resurrection happening at the *last* trumpet, on the *last* day, and Jesus coming back to prove He is the first and the *last*, the beginning and the end (Rev. 1:8, 22:13).

Then Comes the End

> *But now Christ is risen from the dead, and has become the first fruits*
> *of those who have fallen asleep. . . . For as in Adam all die, even so in*
> *Christ all shall be made alive. But each one in his own order: Christ the*

*firstfruits, afterward those who are Christ's at His coming. Then comes
the end.*

—I Corinthians 15:20, 22–24

According to this account, we are resurrected at Christ's coming, verifying once more that there isn't a rapture/resurrection before then. There
also cannot be seven years of tribulation after this resurrection because the
Scripture tells us that when Christ comes, "then comes the end." Christ is
the first and the last; He comes at the last trumpet sound on the last day,
and then it is the end. The Scriptures all work together when we just believe
them.

"It is a righteous thing with God to repay with tribulation those who
trouble you, and to give you who are troubled rest with us when the Lord
Jesus is revealed from heaven with His mighty angels, in flaming fire taking
vengeance on those who do not know God, and on those who do not obey
the gospel of our Lord Jesus Christ. These shall be punished with everlasting destruction from the presence of the Lord and from the glory of His
power, when He comes, in that Day, to be glorified in His saints" (2 Thess.
1:6–10).

Our rest from the tribulations of the world doesn't come by us vanishing in a secret rapture, it comes when Jesus is revealed from heaven. When
something is revealed, it is no longer a secret. "Behold, He is coming with
clouds, and every eye will see Him, even they who pierced Him" (Rev. 1:7).
He's been a secret long enough, and at that day, He will be revealed for who
He is—the Lord of glory! When He is revealed, the ungodly will be punished with an everlasting destruction that will be far worse than seven years
of tribulation.

But the day of the Lord will come as a thief in the night, in which the heavens will pass away with a great noise, and the elements will melt with fervent heat; both the earth and the works that are in it will be burned up. Therefore, since all these things will be dissolved, what manner of persons ought you to be in holy conduct and godliness, looking for and hastening the coming of the day of God, because of which the heavens will be dissolved, being on fire, and the elements will melt with fervent heat? Nevertheless we, according to His promise, look for new heavens and a new earth in which righteousness dwells (2 Pet. 3:10–13).

In 2 Thessalonians 1:7–8, we're told that when the Lord is revealed from heaven, it will be with flaming fire; 2 Peter 3:10-13 encourages the church to look for that day. Why encourage the church to "look" for a day that rapture teachers tell us happens after the rapture? Because the pre-trib theory is completely wrong about a rapture. We need to look for this day as Peter tells us to because what will happen will happen unexpectedly, just as our Lord said.

When our Lord descends from heaven with the sound of the last trumpet, it will not be for a rapture followed by a period of great tribulation. Christ came the first time as Alpha, but when He comes again, it will be as Omega. He was the first, and He will be the last. When Christ descends, it will be at the last day, as time itself will cease and be replaced by eternity. His resurrection power will utterly destroy all death forever. The ungodly will be resurrected to condemnation to be judged and destroyed with fire. The saints shall be resurrected to life and will receive their rewards. The earth will be cleansed with fire and made new. All this happens at the last day, and it will be surprising to us when Jesus appears in the sky for all to see.

Peter told us of the fire that will burn up everything. He said we are to live godly lives and to look for that great fire to come. Those expecting a rapture aren't looking for a global fire—they are looking to disappear long before then.

Jesus started His end-time teaching by talking about a great deception. He said the deception would be so influential that many of His own disciples would be deceived by it. Please make no mistake here—His words are true. The good news is that we don't have to be deceived. The decision is ours, and it depends on whether we hold on to a belief that isn't in the Scriptures or choose to believe what is written in the Word. Choose the Word.

Jesus never promised to rapture us; He promised to come again. He prayed against a rapture, and even told us He would raise all of us at the last day. He also said that both the just and unjust would be raised at that time, with the unjust being removed and thrown in the fire. At that day, every knee shall bow and declare Him Lord. He is the Alpha and Omega, the beginning and the end, and when He comes again, it will be as Omega—the end.